From Club to Catwalk

80s FASH ION

From Club to Catwalk

80s FASHION

Edited by Sonnet Stanfill
V&A Publishing

First published by V&A Publishing, 2013
Victoria and Albert Museum
South Kensington
London SW7 2RL
www.vandapublishing.com

Distributed in North America by Harry N. Abrams Inc., New York
The Board of Trustees of the Victoria and Albert Museum, 2013

ISBN 978 1 85177 725 9
Library of Congress Control Number 2012948896

10 9 8 7 6 5 4 3 2
2017 2016 2015 2014 2013

——

——

Front jacket illustration: Bodymap ensemble using Timney Fowler
textiles, Vogue, August 1984. Photograph by Albert Watson.
Back cover illustration: Design by Helen David for English
Eccentrics, 1984. V&A: 299–1988 (see page 60).
Frontispiece: DJ Jeffrey Hinton and Leigh Bowery at Taboo, London,
1986. Photograph by Mr Hartnett. PYMCA.

Designer: Peter and Paul
Copy-editor: Denny Hemming
Index: Christine Shuttleworth
New photography by Jaron James, V&A Photographic Studio

V&A Publishing
Supporting the world's leading
museum of art and design,
the Victoria and Albert
Museum, London

Contents

The fashions of 1980s London have never really been written about properly. People seem to think that it was only about power dressing and large shoulders pads! But there was much more to it than that. New things were happening in London across the applied arts: fashion, textile design, graphic arts and jewellery design. London's club and music scenes were also closely linked to the city's development as a fashion capital, as were the ground-breaking new fashion and design magazines founded during the decade. This complex, vibrant, London scene is what really sparked young designers' imaginations. The 1980s was a period when many risk-taking young makers were starting out on their own, when their careers really took off. There was so much change! London Fashion Week evolved from a somewhat fragmented affair into an event where designers showed together as a united front. The British government started to take fashion designers seriously for the first time, providing funding, hosting receptions and championing the industry. In business terms, British designers in the 1980s started to sell in significant quantities abroad, to the important markets across Europe and the United States.

In this book, we've aimed to highlight the crossover between fashion and other aspects of London's creative production. We've showcased the work of a wide selection of designers, including some that are not so well known. The V&A, with its vast collections and its many student visitors, is the ideal institution to host this project. I suspect that people will be surprised when they read this book. I hope that they will sense the excitement and experimentation that accompanied the explosion of imaginative talent in 1980s London.

Professor Wendy Dagworthy, OBE
Dean of the School of Material
Head of Fashion Programmes
Royal College of Art, London

FOREWORD

Sarah Whitworth
for New Masters,
Goth prom
ensemble, 1983. V&A:
T.22-24—2012.
Given by Sarah
Whitworth Stuart
and Julia Basnett

Sonnet Stanfill

INTRO DUCT ION

It is with the small, scattered, designer-based independent companies that the verve and refinement of British fashion now resides. [1]

A defining characteristic of 1980s London was the celebration of the independent creator. Whether it was the unsigned new band, the original fashion designer, or the ground-breaking graphic designer, London's embrace of singular artistic vision made it an influential nexus for the creative trinity of music, fashion and design. All were facets of a post-modern culture characterized by experimentation, playful subversion and re-interpretation; striking colour set against stark black-and-white graphics, historical quotations and a layering of complexity. The prevailing atmosphere was one of creative symbiosis. Clubs morphed into catwalks, and style magazines mediated the cultural mix. New careers emerged, from pop stylists and video makers to independent music producers and art directors. For many, the 1980s were the glory days.

And London was the creative hub. One designer summed up London's ability to act as a catalyst:

The club scene meant that people used to dress up. It was that whole London scene that was so vibrant; that's what really started young designers going. The art college students used to go to these clubs straight from college—you worked hard but you played hard too. London's rebellious atmosphere: I think that's what pushed us forward. [2]

The capital attracted talent of all kinds: the self-taught and the art-school trained, creative collaborators and rogue retailers. The generation of London-based designers who came to prominence during the 1980s included the optimistic, ambitious graduates of the city's renowned art colleges such as the Royal College of Art, St Martin's School of Art and London College of Fashion, as well as the former Hornsey College in Crouch End and Chelsea School of Art. [3] New hot spots of vibrant commerce played a vital part in London's successful transformation into an international fashion capital, one that encouraged entrepreneurial effort and risk-taking design. From the late 1970s, designers and retailers had been opening stores in diverse locations across London: Paul Smith's shop on Floral Street was instrumental in establishing Covent Garden's reputation as a fashion retail location; Pam Hogg's shop energized Newburgh Street, near Oxford Circus; Modern Classics in Rivington Street, Shoreditch, was, recalled a former client, 'deeply embedded in the first colonization of the East End' (01), [4] and collective markets such as Hyper Hyper on Kensington High Street became shopping destinations.

01 ⌄
Trade card for Modern Classics, Willy Brown's store in Shoreditch. V&A archives. Given by Philip Hoare

If the Swinging Sixties put London fashion on the map, the 1980s saw designer fashion (as opposed to mass manufacture) mature into a commercially viable enterprise. Many influential contributors helped realise the creation of a more orderly and effective system of promoting designer fashion, and a number of professional organizations arose to encourage the industry. The Incorporated Society of London Designers, founded in the early 1940s, was followed by the London Designer Collections (LDC) founded in 1974 and the Individual Clothes Show (ICS) founded a few years later. They were joined in 1983 by the British Fashion Council (BFC). [5] The key protagonists of these organisations included Annette Worsley-Taylor, Wendy Booth, Lynne Franks and Lesley Goring. Although fragmented and lagging behind their counterparts in cities like Paris and Milan, these bodies helped to establish the necessary infrastructure for modern fashion displays, catwalk shows and selling events at various locations throughout the capital. Furthermore, while Britain's early clothing trade fairs were aimed squarely at the middle and mass markets, by the early years of the 1980s, the activities of these organizations brought an acceptance of high end British designer labels. The work of the LDC, ICS and BFC established the infrastructure of what we recognise as London Fashion Week. This infrastructure included organised press and promotion, a more carefully orchestrated social calendar that offered receptions for buyers and other visitors, and ultimately, by the mid-1980s, the establishment of a single, main location for catwalk shows along with one runway show schedule for each season. These efforts brought success: by the decade's end, British designer fashion represented the country's fifth largest industrial sector, worth £6 billion and accounting for 9 per cent of the manufacturing workforce.[6]

The LDC, ICS and the BFC were essential in the successful promotion of London fashion to journalists and buyers, both at home and abroad. Proof of their efficacy was the constant stream of international visitors to the seasonal collections. The BBC's launch of the successful television programme *The Clothes Show* in 1986 further confirmed that London fashion was news. From the *New York Times* to Japan's *Mainichi Shimbun*, reporters were regularly dispatched to London to cover its catwalk shows. Further, these organizations helped secure vital business and government support for the British fashion industry. With their encouragement, the government became more directly involved with fashion. Margaret Thatcher, Prime Minister from 1979 to 1990, hosted multiple Downing Street receptions for the sector. Thatcher summarized the significance of fashion for Britain by declaring, 'Fashion is important because it raises the quality of life when people take the trouble to dress well and it also provides employment for many, many people.' [7]

While London's fashion industry became more professional, the city retained its anarchic reputation. A fashion journalist from Ohio reported in 1989 with exasperation, 'It was late, it was dark and of course it was raining on our first day in London for the British fashion collections, and look where designer Rifat Ozbek was sending us – to some Godforsaken barn of a recording studio that was indeed, as our concerned doorman had warned, in an unsavoury part of town.'[8] Contemporary foreign press reports frequently described London street scenes for added flavour. The *Sunday Oklahoma* reported in 1986, 'Punk Rock hairstyles and clothes that look like rejects from a 1960s shop on Carnaby Street still lurk about on London streets, providing dashes of humor and vicarious experiences into the underground of London fashion'. [9] That same year, the *Dallas Morning News* enquired, 'What would London be without its punk-packed shows featuring everything from Mad Max hairdos to medieval-inspired rags?'[10]

Surprisingly, perhaps, the evolution of London's designer fashion sector was taking place against a stark backdrop of social unrest. For much of the 1980s, terrorist bombings, miners' strikes and high unemployment preoccupied the nation, as did the rise of HIV/AIDS. Of this tumultuous period Thatcher later wrote, 'For a moment, it seemed as if rationality and decency would go under.'[11] Yet dramatic changes implemented by the Thatcher government (industry deregulation, more flexible labour markets, the privatization of state-owned companies and a reduction of trade union power) resulted in an economic climate favourable to entrepreneurs across a number of industries from the high profile music and advertising sectors to fashion.

02 →
Betty Jackson, ensemble from the Spring/Summer 1985 collection in the window of Saks Fifth Avenue, New York, 1985. Collection of Wendy Dagworthy

The success of these enterprises often depended on establishing overseas markets, something that the BFC and its related organizations helped to facilitate for the fashion industry. Throughout the decade, Americans in particular emerged as enthusiastic consumers of London's designer fashion. Explosive growth on Wall Street drove the prosperity of the Reagan years, and encouraged sales of British fashion in the United States. After the success of Mary Quant in the 1960s (her collaboration with mass-market retailer J.C. Penney placed her designs in most of their 1700 stores across the country) and the defiant, mould-breaking styles of late 1970s punk, American buyers continued to look to London for fresh, new designs. When stores such as Macy's and Saks Fifth Avenue sent buyers to London shows, their sizable orders could be career-defining. After several years of courting overseas buyers, by 1985, 40 per cent of Betty Jackson's business and 60 per cent of Wendy Dagworthy's came from American sales of their clothing.[12] Said Jackson, 'Some of us travelled to New York, where we visited Saks, Neiman Marcus, Nordstrom and I. Magnin and did trunk shows. It was huge. We did £40,000 to £50,000 per season in the US at that time' (02). [13]

In addition to the United States, Pacific Rim countries such as Japan and Australia extended the reach of London's designer creations. In 1984, boutique owner and club impresario Suzanne Bartsch staged two shows of London fashion in New York. Later that year, she took a group of 20 London designers to Tokyo: Rachel Auburn, Betty Jackson, Leigh Bowery, Sue Clowes, John Richmond, Crolla (Scott Crolla and Georgina Godley), Koje Tatsuko for Culture Shock, Gregory Davis, Dean Bright, Elmaz Huseyin, Memento (Janice Hall and Bruno Broniecki), Helen Littman (later Helen David, English Eccentrics' founder), Richard Torry, Dexter Wong, milliners Stephen Jones and Bernstock Speirs, jewellery designer Judy Blame, along with art director Michael Costiff (04). Artwork was by Trojan (03).

Though the event, titled *London Goes to Tokyo*, heralded London's international reputation, it illustrated the still amateur status of its fashion system. Delivered on a shoestring budget, there was an atmosphere of jovial disorder. Betty Jackson recalled an awkward press conference held for designers who were 'unprepared and naïve'. [14] Photographer and filmmaker-turned designer Michael Costiff recollected cash-strapped participants stocking up on food at the hotel breakfast table, and arguments about hair and make-up for models that resulted in Leigh Bowery finally securing the theatrical, clown-like face paint he wanted, against the wishes of other designers. [15]

What *London Goes to Tokyo* lacked in polish, it made up for in panache. The designers staged six catwalk presentations over two days to a packed hall on the fifth floor of Tokyo's Hanae Mori Building. A flyer urged the curious to 'Come see for yourselves as 20 of Britain's top young designers display their collections'. The same leaflet boasted, 'This year London is the hub of hot new fashion, music, video and art. Don't miss out!'

While a number of designers flirted with Japan, opening shops and then closing them soon after, Paul Smith was about to arrange a business venture that would change the course of his company. In 1982, his reputation growing, a Japanese businessman had invited him to visit Japan. Two years later, he opened his first shop there. Gradually, Japan became an important source of sales for Smith, who credits cultural curiosity and a commitment to regular travel for his success:

> **I think the reason why my business has become so successful in Japan is because I worked at it. I must have been at least 80 times: four times a year for many years. I have tried to learn their culture, understand their way of life, understand their market. And I never complain about the jetlag, or the economy seats, or the hotel. In the early days it was just exciting to go! Slowly, slowly, slowly it has built into a very substantial business, and a business that has a foundation.** [16]

04 →
Designers featured in the <u>London Goes to Tokyo</u> show, including Stephen Jones (second row, third from right), Betty Jackson (front row, far right) and John Richmond (third row, far right). <u>W Japan</u>, November 1984. Courtesy of Betty Jackson

Alongside the commercial development of London's fashion industry in the 1980s, however, a notable divide emerged between 'establishment' fashion designers – those creating traditional day and evening clothing for women of means – and the more rebellious approach of the so-called 'street' designers. Milliner Stephen Jones's reflections on *London Goes to Tokyo* illustrate this dilemma:

> **[It] was a huge cultural thing for the Japanese. I don't think they had really seen fashion like this presented on the catwalk. I've spoken to Japanese designers since and they said that for them, the idea of 'street fashion' didn't really exist. They used the word 'street fashion' at that time, which we disliked because we wanted to be real fashion designers. We considered ourselves to be real fashion designers, as opposed to this funny thing that came off the street. We were all very much individuals. Everybody on that list was showing different things.** [17]

The wedding of Prince Charles to Lady Diana Spencer on 29 July 1981 provided the high-end designers with a serendipitous boost. Princess Diana became an important supporter of London fashion, regularly wearing the clothes of Jacques Azagury, Jasper Conran, Bruce Oldfield, Catherine Walker and many others (05). On her royal tour of Australia in the spring of 1983 the Princess packed outfits by no less than 21 different designers. *Harpers & Queen* reported that of Diana's selected designers, 'None of them could conceivably be seen as fighting in the front line of any style war. Instead they specialize in very pretty, very sensible, very smart, utterly Sloaney stuff ... Charming, appropriate and definitely not innovative'.[18] The Princess's wardrobe choices, while not at fashion's cutting edge, nonetheless set styles and made headlines.

05 ↓
Diana, Princess of Wales, and Bruce Oldfield at a charity event at Grosvenor House Hotel, London, November 1988

In contrast, numerous other London designers aimed for subversion. These iconoclasts were championed by a new crop of trend-setting boutiques and markets, important among them being Hyper Hyper (06). It was here, on the New Masters stand, that Sarah Whitworth sold her collections, including a Goth prom ensemble with skeleton print, designed in 1983 (07). Lou, a manageress at Hyper Hyper, relates that she sold the ensemble to 'debs who wanted a different type of ballgown', and describes its appeal as 'a feminine look, but it's not soppy. Why should a woman look sweet and pliable just because men want us to look that way? ... It's aggressively seductive. Let's not reassure men. Let's scare 'em! [19]

Whitworth was just one of many London-based designers working within the realm of clothing and textiles but outside the mainstream fashion system. This was certainly true of Australian-born performance artist Leigh Bowery, who, as fashion historian Rebecca Arnold has written, 'used clothing and make-up as a means to construct visions of the extreme'. [20] Bowery had started out making clothes for himself and his friends. The fashion collection he took to the *London Goes to Tokyo* catwalk show was one of his last. Its somewhat shoddily constructed, layered ensembles verged on costume, harbingers of his later notorious stage creations (08, 09).

06 ↓
Hyper Hyper
poster, 1982.
V&A: E.575—2012.
Given by Sarah
Whitworth Stuart

07 ↓
**Sarah Whitworth
for New Masters,
Goth prom ensemble,
1983. V&A: T.22-
24—2012.
Given by Sarah
Whitworth Stuart
and Julia Basnett**

08 →
**Leigh Bowery, ensemble
of white nylon trimmed
with brown, floral printed
cotton, 1984.
V&A: 63:1-2—2009**

Suzy Menkes, fashion editor for the *International Herald Tribune*, implored, 'Will London fashion designers ever be able to capture the street spirit in their shows? Or are they forever destined to divide between the wild and the tame – one lot making news and the other dressing Princess Diana?' [21] Summing up London's split personality, the *Toronto Star* stated:

> **If the clothes look like something Diana, Princess of Wales might wear, chances are the designer has his or her feet planted firmly on the side of the establishment. If, on the other hand, the clothes come off looking a bit wacky or witty or outrageous then you can bet that the designer is of the other school, one of the inimitable British 'street' designers who create attention-getting fashion.' [22]**

09 ↓
Leigh Bowery, ensemble shown at <u>London Goes to Tokyo</u>, 1984.

The dichotomy of London's fashion production continually challenged the fashion press, resulting in evolving fashion coverage and the founding of influential new magazines. As the decade progressed, orthodox fashion vehicles such as British *Vogue* seemed ever more out of step with the events gripping the nation. As the divisive miners' strike worsened, *Vogue's* May 1984 issue hit the newsstands with a cover featuring a soft-focus photograph of a pastel-clad model surrounded by the words, 'Charm! The most appealing way to look now'. [23] The September issue that year included advice on the so-called 'new' direction in eveningwear titled 'Twinsets and Pearls'. This left the door wide open for more cutting-edge publications, such as *The Face*, founded by *New Musical Express* editor Nick Logan in 1980, and *i-D*, founded that same year by former *Vogue* art director Terry Jones. Together, *The Face* and *i-D* celebrated the raw creativity in fashion and music of London's youth culture, while *Blitz* (1980–91) focused on media and popular culture. Further, in response to the lack of mainstream British press interest in its home-grown designers, the launch of British *Elle* in November 1985 aimed to capture the dynamism and diversity of Britain's designer fashion. The rallying cry of Sally Brampton, *Elle's* first editor, was to 'Stamp out Sloanes!' [24]

London fashion had a wild ride in the 1980s. It was the decade when civil unrest threatened to undermine the country's social order. The economic climate, in which the creative sector had initially flourished, then faltered with the stock market crash of October 1987, which saw the dollar's strength against the pound decline by over 25 per cent. [25] Such volatility (combined in some cases, it must be said, with youthful impetuousness) forced many designer businesses to close. The somewhat amateurish, ad hoc approach that marked the fashion industry in the early 1980s was echoed in the anarchic working environment of the music production companies, and of the nightclubs that sprang up spontaneously across the capital. New and sympathetic modes of presentation in style magazines were marked by a DIY, cut-and-paste aesthetic, which embraced the seemingly accidental. Yet by the end of the decade, the 'dressed-up to excess' ethos of the earlier club scene had evolved into a more relaxed, informal look; style magazines had moved on to become more commercial propositions; London had reasserted itself as a credible source of stylistically sophisticated, well crafted and promoted designer fashion. The 1980s generation had grown up.

Revisiting the decade from the perspective of the twenty-first century, this book, and the exhibition that it accompanies, is a timely reappraisal of a creative period that is often dismissed or misunderstood. Within the context of the nightclub, the catwalk and the magazine spread, the essays that follow illustrate the convergence of music, fashion and design that characterized the times. Contributions include 'New Styles New Sounds', which explores London's club-centred street culture, a demotic mix of music and fashion; 'London Calling', which examines the broader fashion spectrum, from street to high end production; and 'Irony and Mythology', which looks at fashion through the innovative graphic design and imagery adopted by the newly-arrived 'style' magazines. A selection of fashion accessories illustrates the details of fashionable choice. Central to the story, of course, are the voices of the makers themselves, represented here by Wendy Dagworthy, OBE and Sir Paul Smith.

Daniel Milford-Cottam

Jewellery offered the opportunity for bold style statements, from sculptural bangles to chunky necklaces to oversized earrings. Norman Parkinson photographed Iman, flawlessly made-up, wearing dramatic Butler & Wilson costume jewellery, a saucy Graham Smith hat and seemingly little else, for the fashion-themed 1985 Pirelli Calendar. The calendar, produced annually since 1964, typically features artistic nude or semi-nude 'glamour' images taken by leading photographers. For the 1985 edition, Pirelli approached a number of established British designers, including Bruce Oldfield and Zandra Rhodes, to create garments and accessories incorporating Pirelli's distinctive tyre-track motif. The designers rose to the challenge with great ingenuity. Graham Smith ran the track across the sheer nylon mesh of his hat, whilst Butler & Wilson picked out the design in black-and-white pavé diamanté.

Accessory

BUTLER & WILSON / GRAHAM SMITH FOR PIRELLI

10
Graham Smith hat and Butler & Wilson paste jewellery, 1984.
V&A: T.479–1985; T.469, 470&A, 472, 473–1985

11
Pirelli Calendar, 1985.
Modelled by Iman, photograph by Norman Parkinson

Johnny Moke opened his London shoe boutique on the King's Road in 1984. He was a self-taught designer who created his first footwear in the late 1970s and became known for his clever mixes of fabric, finishes and decorative devices. Moke disliked flat shoes, so unusual heels became one of his trademarks, such as his 1986 'Egg Heel', which presented the surrealistic impression of a woman balancing upon two white eggs. Another typical design was the 'Golden Ball' slingback for Summer 1990, where three gilded balls supported a classic hot pink satin slingback. His witty, sophisticated footwear catered to wearers who appreciated a touch of originality but were conservative enough to shy away from the more uncompromising shoe designs of the decade.

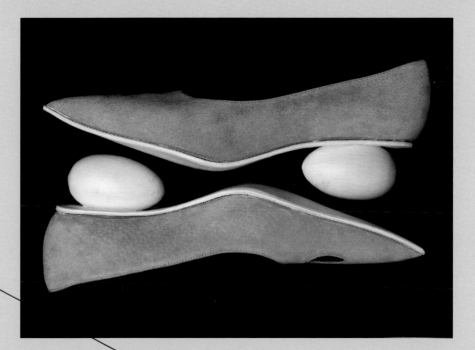

JOHNNY MOKE

12
Johnny Moke for Adeline André, women's
'Egg Heel' shoes, 1986.
V&A: T.235&A–1990

Designer Statement

WENDY DAGWORTHY

13 ↗
**Wendy Dagworthy
in the V&A storeroom
with her designs, 2011**

I never had an official launch. I never thought, 'Right, I'm going to start my own company'. It just gradually happened. Prudence Glynn, who was Fashion Editor of <u>The Times</u>, came to my show in 1971, liked my collection and recommended me to a company called Radley, who backed Ossie Clark at that time, and they took me on as a womenswear designer.

I started making my own clothes as well and used to make clothes for my friends. Through one of them I met Bryan Ferry, and I did some stage outfits for him and for Phil Manzanera, which was great as a little sideline. An early specialty of mine was initialled shirts – I remember making some initialled pyjamas for Bryan Ferry (I think he had had his tonsils out) and that was the start of it all. Through the Roxy Music collaboration we met other groups, such as Kevin Godley and Lol Creme from 10cc; and then Pete Townshend and Roger Daltrey from The Who. As we used to sell to Harvey Nichols, Harrods and Liberty, some of the Royals wore my clothes as well.

In 1972, I started cutting down the number of days I spent working for other people to concentrate on my own line. Countdown, a boutique on the King's Road, bought a few of my designs, and I thought, 'If Countdown like my collection, maybe others will, too'. I approached shops like Universal Witness and Che Guevara, and they all bought. I remember the first Big Order, which was from Che Guevara and was, I think, for £1500 – a lot of money in those days.

In 1973, Betty Jackson came to work with me. At that point I used to have a workroom in the flat. I didn't use factories, I wasn't big enough. I would cut everything out on a table, then take it round to my machinists, who worked all over London. They used to make up the orders and then my husband and I, or Betty and I, would travel round collecting these made-up garments. Then, they'd have to be buttonholed and delivered to the shops. It was very cottage-industry. At that time there was only myself, Betty, one freelance pattern-cutter and one machinist.

The challenge of those early days was always cash flow. What you earned on one collection, you put into the next. Another challenge was production – any delay could result in cancelled orders. A further difficulty was achieving a consistent standard of making. You had to ensure quality control. If something wasn't well made, you'd get returns.

So many early developments happened through word of mouth. It was through my buttonholer Eve, in Berwick Street, that we got the floor above her that became my first studio or showroom. And because Eve used to do everyone's buttonholes, she knew other factories. That's how, when I expanded, I was able to make the transition from outworkers to factory production.

In terms of the design process, as a fashion designer, you always start with the cloth first.

My whole thing was quite eclectic. We used to go to Interstoff, the big fabric fair in Frankfurt. I'd combine Indian fabrics with maybe an Italian fabric or a Spanish fabric and British as well, especially for winter collections. For the Autumn/Winter 1982 collection I had used Irish tweeds from a company called Aran Tweed in Ireland's Aran Islands. They flew me out there on a special visit. We arrived by a tiny propeller plane and landed in a field; the fabrics were woven in people's houses, like crofters, and used to be delivered by boat, with cattle on it – you wondered how it ever got to you.

I used to buy from India, too, and used a lot of ikats. In 1985 I went on a visit to the textile company and the villages where the fabrics were being made. What I liked about the Indian fabrics was the fact that they weren't perfect. You'd find a bit of straw in one, or you'd find that the tension would change in another, where someone else had taken over the loom in the afternoon. Each season I'd meet representatives from the company and we'd go through the different fabrics. We'd decide on colourways and build up the selection that I wanted in that collection. As you are selecting the fabrics, you're thinking about the collection at the same time. Then, I'd design it. I would spend a few days at home just concentrating, researching and thinking.

Once I'd designed the collection, I'd show it at London Designer Collections, take the orders and add them up. Then the bulk fabric would be ordered, and once it had arrived it would be sent out to the different factories to be made up. The garments would then come back to us, bagged and ready to go, and we'd pack the boxes and deliver them. It was often quite tight, the turnaround time. I remember carrying boxes to the post office together – in those days everyone helped when time was tight.

14 →
**Wendy Dagworthy
fashion sketch,
Spring/Summer
1985 collection.
Courtesy Wendy
Dagworthy**

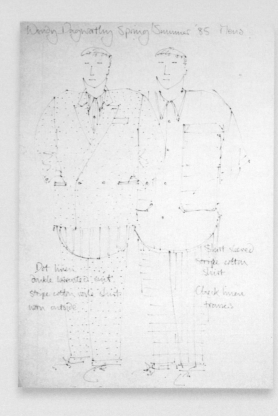

An inspiration for this collection was an old man's dress shirt, from which I copied details such as the detachable collar, and I showed long johns worn under skirts or dresses.

In 1974, a group of us, led by Annette Worsley-Taylor, had set up the London Designer Collections (LDC), at a time when there was no platform for designers in London. Until this point, it had all been mainly about the rag trade's shows at Earls Court at one end and couture at the other. London's designer fashion had been more about eveningwear – there weren't so many daywear designers. Also, coming out of the 1960s, there were boutiques and little shops; you didn't really wholesale then. When we started LDC we used to mail out to stores in America and Italy, as well as London. Then their buyers started coming to us. That was when wholesale began and when London became truly an international fashion city. Before these efforts, those buyers were non-existent.

A year or so earlier, I had met Lynne Franks. She was very helpful in getting me press, and she'd only just started herself. She had people like Katharine Hamnett on her books. She went on to be my PR for the whole 16 years I was in business, and we're still friends. She was instrumental in saying, 'You've got to have a show!' I felt I'd really made it when I had my first: Spring/Summer 1979. It was a 9.30 breakfast show at the Playboy Club. I think we had Bucks Fizz and croissants, which the Bunny Girls served.

By this time, we'd stopped using machinists in their homes. We had been introduced to a tailor, who used to do all our tailoring as well as heavier outerwear, and he had a small factory. We carried on using small factories nearby in Berwick Street, where we had our premises. After a few years of economic slump, from 1983 sales started increasing again with orders coming in from across Britain, Europe and the United States.

My Spring/Summer 1985 collection was bought by Saks Fifth Avenue as part of a celebration of British fashion. There was Betty Jackson, Reubeen Tariq and myself. It was really fantastic and we were well received. At that time we were selling to stores all over America, including Henri Bendel and Barneys in New York and Maxfield Blue in Los Angeles. Saks sent me a photo album showing our clothes in the windows. We also had collections in-store, displayed with the British flag flying, and there were in-store catwalk shows. We did press interviews – it was really well organized. We must have been selling to about 50 shops in Italy as well. The collection that season had a mix of Irish linens in various stripes and a selection of Liberty prints, both a larger print and one of the classic small floral prints. At this period, we were still producing in small factories but in the north of England, in places like Nottingham. We never manufactured overseas.

An inspiration for this collection was an old man's dress shirt, from which I copied details such as the detachable collar, and I showed long johns worn under skirts or dresses. Menswear has been a constant reference for me in many of my collections. I'm not a girly designer.

For the Spring/Summer 1987 collections, a group of us made a special trip to New York: Betty Jackson, Katharine Hamnett, John Galliano, Jasper Conran, Bodymap (they showed separately) and me. British designers, en masse.

We were very professional about it. We had a PR to promote us. We had someone booking buying appointments. We all took suites in a hotel and we sold from there. We had a party at Little Nells, which was the groovy club at the time. I remember Katharine and I went

15 ↘
Wendy Dagworthy,
ensemble featured in
the London Designer
Collections catalogue,
Autumn/Winter 1982

PERRY OGDEN

Wendy Dagworthy

Looking back, in terms of the 1980s as a decade, what was important to my success as a London designer was the fantastic club and music scene, which coincided with the careers of so many young designers.

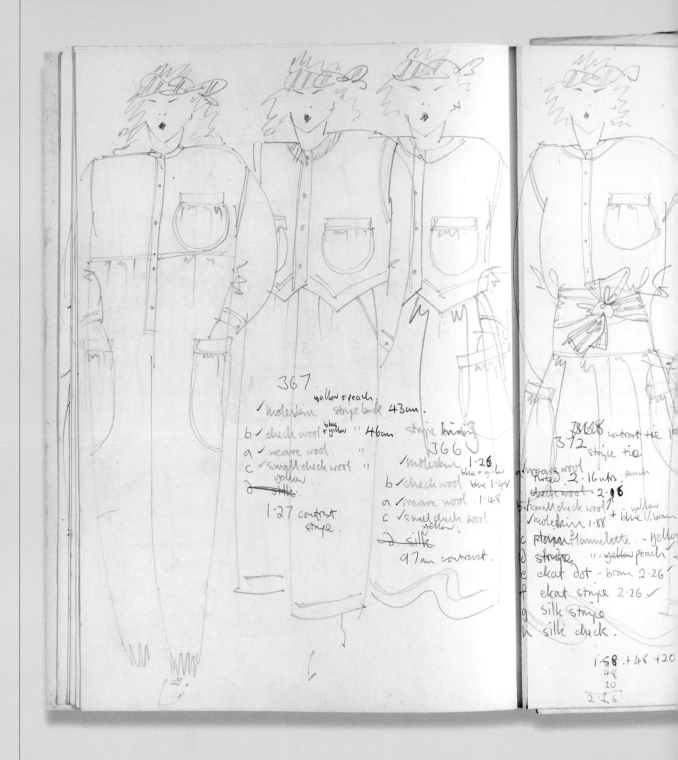

on morning TV. We had lots of press and we sold really well. Then we did it again the next year for the Autumn/Winter 1987 collection. I think we felt the good times would go on forever. I wish!

We sold, delivered, and then – that's when it hit. Black Monday in the United States, in October 1987, changed things dramatically: America stopped coming to buy, Italy stopped coming to buy and it was a difficult time for lots of designers. The end, for me, came all at once. By the next year I'd closed my business and begun a new career in fashion education.

Looking back, in terms of the 1980s as a decade, what was important to my success as a London designer was the fantastic club and music scene, which coincided with the careers of so many young designers. There were a lot more young designer companies then, and there were new exhibitions like the Individual Clothes Show, Amalgamated Talent and Design Studio. All this gave London a real sense of excitement. London design is experimental. It doesn't conform, it has its own look. I think our designers are very individual, thanks to our art college education. American art colleges have a different perspective, as do Italian art colleges. It's more commercial, more focused on industry. In London, it's freer.

We encourage students to challenge and push the boundaries. When I started my own collection, I wanted to do what I REALLY believed in. And speaking as the Head of Fashion at the Royal College of Art, that's what we encourage our students to do as well. Have the confidence to create what you really believe in.

What also made a difference to me as a designer in 1980s London was the government's interest in its own fashion industry. Margaret Thatcher hosted a reception for the fashion sector at Downing Street in 1983. The British Fashion Council was founded around that time and, from then on, the government became more directly involved, helping to fund London Fashion Week. Later in the decade the Princess of Wales invited fashion designers to Lancaster House for receptions. We began to have big parties for 700 people with VIPs attending. Finally, fashion was really being taken seriously.

16 ↖
Wendy Dagworthy
fashion sketch,
Autumn/Winter
1982 collection.
Courtesy Wendy
Dagworthy

Daniel Milford-Cottam

As the 1980s drew to a close, designers increasingly embraced multicultural and multi-ethnic fabrics, styles and craftsmanship, which were combined with familiar garment forms to create a completely fresh approach. Atelier, founded by Julian Brogden in 1984, was a jewellery and fashion metalwork company. Working out of a disused hospital in Hackney alongside fellow designers Judy Blame and Slim Barrett, Brogden and his business partner Cathy Jordan produced jewellery and accessories with metalwork elements, including sculptural shoe heels, decorative clips, and even body armour for Vivienne Westwood. Towards the end of the decade they diversified into headwear, creating hats for Duran Duran and Diana, Princess of Wales. Their black felt bowler hat features a thin shell of pierced, engraved and silver-plated brass across the domed crown. The traditional, quintessentially British bowler is subverted by this exquisitely wrought metalwork.

Accessory

ATELIER

17
Atelier, black felt bowler hat, 1989.
V&A: T.176–1990. Given by Atelier

Sock Shop was envisioned by its founder Sophie Mirman as somewhere people could buy fun, moderately priced socks, in unusual designs, colours and patterns, 'as easily as they buy newspapers'.[1] Prior to its launch in 1983, most British socks and hosiery were mass-produced in conservative styles and retailed by department stores. From modest beginnings in London's Knightsbridge tube station, Sock Shop rapidly grew to include outlets in railway stations, airports and shopping centres across Europe and the United States. The success of this business model was imitated by other product-specific businesses such as Tie Rack and the shirt-makers T.M.Lewin. By the late 1980s, many leading British designers including Jane Gottelier from Artwork, Helen Storey and English Eccentrics were producing exclusive hosiery designs for Sock Shop. Some, such as Workers for Freedom, also designed complementary product packaging.

SOCK SHOP

18
*Sock Shop, socks and tights featuring designs by Jane Gottelier,
Helen Storey, Workers For Freedom and English Eccentrics, 1989–90.
V&A: T.14–1990, T.178–1991, T.21–1990, T.15–1990 and T.17–1990*

Note: 1 Steve Lohr, 'A "Silly" Sock Idea Makes Millions', *New York Times*, 23 November 1987.

NEW
STYLE
NEWS

Part 01

**Clubbing, Music and Fashion
in 1980s London** / Shaun Cole

**TALES
NEW
SOUNDS**

We see people brand new people, They're something to see, We're nightclubbing.

'Nightclubbing', David Bowie and Iggy Pop, 1977

In his 1980 video *Ashes to Ashes* David Bowie, clad in a glittering Pierrot costume designed by Natasha Korniloff, is accompanied by four other strikingly garbed characters. They had been plucked the night before from London's already notorious Blitz nightclub in Great Queen Street. One was the Blitz's host, Steve Strange, who wore a black wedding dress and lace veil headdress that he had bought from designer Judith Frankland following her Ravensbourne College graduation show. The others were Frankland and fashion designer Darla-Jane Gilroy, both attired in the ecclesiastic-style outfits they had worn to the club the previous night, and fellow Blitz habitué Elise (19). Just as musician and style icon Bowie had inspired young musicians, designers and clubbers to express themselves creatively through their clothing, using the nightclub as their arena, so the nightclub founded to play Bowie's music in turn provided the stylistic inspiration for his video.

19 →
Judith Frankland, wearing one of her ecclesiastic-style designs, at Blitz, London, August 1980. Photograph by Graham Smith

This focus on creative self-expression formed the ethos of London clubs in the early 1980s, with young people making innovative statements about contemporary life through their dress. Jumble sale finds, home-sewn ensembles and theatrical costumes were worn along with clothes bought from Seditionaries/Worlds End (established by Malcolm McLaren with subsequent assistance from Vivienne Westwood), PX (set up by Stephane Raynor and Helen Robinson, and where Strange had been a shop assistant), Modern Classics (run by Willy Brown and Vivienne Lynn) and Jon Baker's emporium Axiom, which sold designs by those who frequented these very clubs.

In her 2011 book *Music and Fashion* Janice Miller identifies 'the role that fashion and clothing could play in maintaining and articulating a cultural identity' [1] and draws on Italian academic Patrizia Calefato's observation that fashion and music are 'two social practices that go hand in hand ... drawing on a common sensibility which translates into taste' and have 'always used citations, experiences, influences and suggestions taken from the past'. [2] Sociologist Sarah Thornton has also stated that 'club cultures are taste cultures' and that the people who go to clubs do so on the basis of a shared taste in music or style. [3] The discussion of London nightclubs as a site for the interaction between music and clothing has previously occurred within the lens of subcultural practice. [4] This chapter is neither an attempt to analyze and address particular subcultural practices, nor is it an in-depth record of the development of London's clubs (21 illustrates the complexity of this network). Instead, it provides a series of snapshots of the arenas in which music and fashion freely collided. As designer, and later lead singer of the group Blue Rondo à la Turk, Chris Sullivan has noted, 'if clothing was our most immediate form of expression, then the club was where we exhibited it'. [5]

London's nightclubs, like their clientele, established their own identities through styles of music and presentation that were uniquely integral to each. Nods to historicism were a common factor, made through a juxtaposition of retro music and the clothing of their habitués. Thursday nights at Hell in Henrietta Street reflected the darker, decorative elements of the venue in religious-styled clothes by young designers such as Fiona Dealey and Stephen Linard, who both graduated from Saint Martin's School of Art, Linard with his *Neo Gothic* collection in 1980. This Gothic aesthetic was taken to an extreme at The Batcave, held at the Gargoyle Club on Dean Street, which opened as an outlet for the band Specimen, and was hosted by its lead singer Ollie Wisdom, 'a Jaggeresque youth in mascara and black lace'. [6] The dress style of the members of Specimen and other Batcave clubbers mixed the darker side of 1970s glam with historic styling derived from horror films and elements of fetishwear (20). Shops such as Symphony of Shadows in Hyper Hyper on Kensington High Street, run by Laurie Vanian, wife of the lead singer of the band The Damned, sold black and purple velvet, lace and leather clothes that were combined with 'deathly' make-up and dyed black, backcombed hair. The term Goth(ic) applied equally to music as to style and Hamish McDonald, DJ at The Batcave, described the music he played as 'a sweeping curve of sound, with Siouxsie and the Cramps as middle ground, taking in Sweet and the Specimen and stretching to Eddie Cochran and Death Cult'. [7] On Tuesdays at Le Kilt in Greek Street, a 1940s and 50s suited elegance took over, the exaggerated zoot suits of Sullivan reflecting the pre-punk funk, jazz and Latin sounds that were played there (22).

20 →
BOY advertisement featuring Johnny Slut, keyboard player in the Gothic group Specimen, i-D, no. 14, 1983

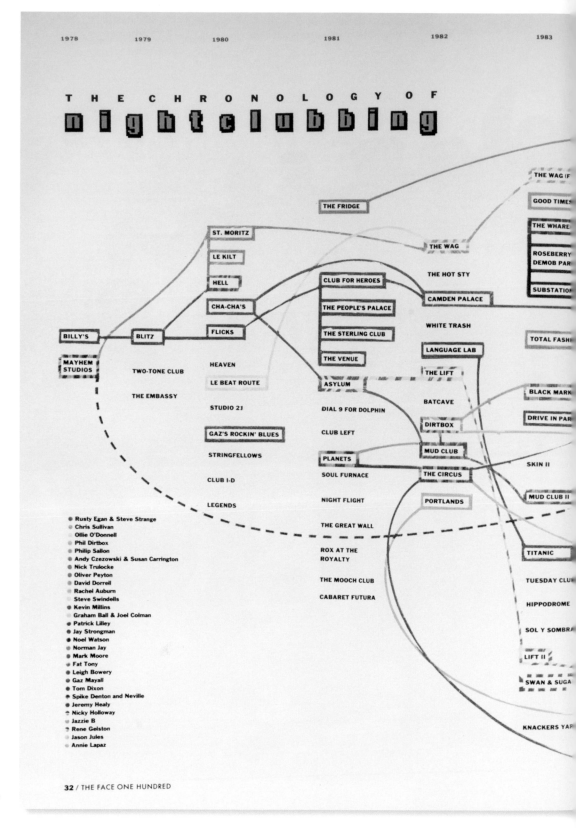

THE CHRONOLOGY OF
nightclubbing

1978   1979   1980   1981   1982   1983

THE WAG (F

GOOD TIMES

THE WHARE

THE FRIDGE

ST. MORITZ   THE WAG   ROSEBERRY
                                                                DEMOB PAR
LE KILT   CLUB FOR HEROES   THE HOT STY
                                                                SUBSTATION
HELL   CAMDEN PALACE
                                 THE PEOPLE'S PALACE
CHA-CHA'S
                                 THE STERLING CLUB   WHITE TRASH   TOTAL FASHI
BILLY'S   BLITZ   FLICKS
                                 THE VENUE   LANGUAGE LAB
MAYHEM   THE LIFT
STUDIOS   TWO-TONE CLUB   HEAVEN   ASYLUM   BLACK MARK
                                 LE BEAT ROUTE
          THE EMBASSY   BATCAVE   DRIVE IN PAR
                                 STUDIO 21   DIAL 9 FOR DOLPHIN
                                                                    DIRTBOX
                 GAZ'S ROCKIN' BLUES   CLUB LEFT
                                                     MUD CLUB
                 STRINGFELLOWS   PLANETS   SKIN II
                                        SOUL FURNACE THE CIRCUS
                 CLUB I-D
                                        NIGHT FLIGHT PORTLANDS   MUD CLUB II
                 LEGENDS
⦿ Rusty Egan & Steve Strange   THE GREAT WALL
⦿ Chris Sullivan
⦿ Ollie O'Donnell   ROX AT THE   TITANIC
⦿ Phil Dirtbox   ROYALTY
⦿ Philip Sallon
⦿ Andy Czezowski & Susan Carrington THE MOOCH CLUB   TUESDAY CLU
⦿ Nick Trulocke
⦿ Oliver Peyton   CABARET FUTURA   HIPPODROME
⦿ David Dorrell
⦿ Rachel Auburn   SOL Y SOMBRA
⦿ Steve Swindells
⦿ Kevin Millins   LIFT II
⦿ Graham Ball & Joel Colman
⦿ Patrick Lilley
⦿ Jay Strongman   SWAN & SUGA
⦿ Noel Watson
⦿ Norman Jay
⦿ Mark Moore
⦿ Fat Tony
⦿ Leigh Bowery
⦿ Gaz Mayall   KNACKERS YAR
⦿ Tom Dixon
⦿ Spike Denton and Neville
⦿ Jeremy Healy
⦿ Nicky Holloway
⦿ Jazzie B
⦿ Rene Gelston
⦿ Jason Jules
⦿ Annie Lapaz

21 →
***'The Chronology
of Nightclubbing',***
The Face, *no. 100,
September 1988*

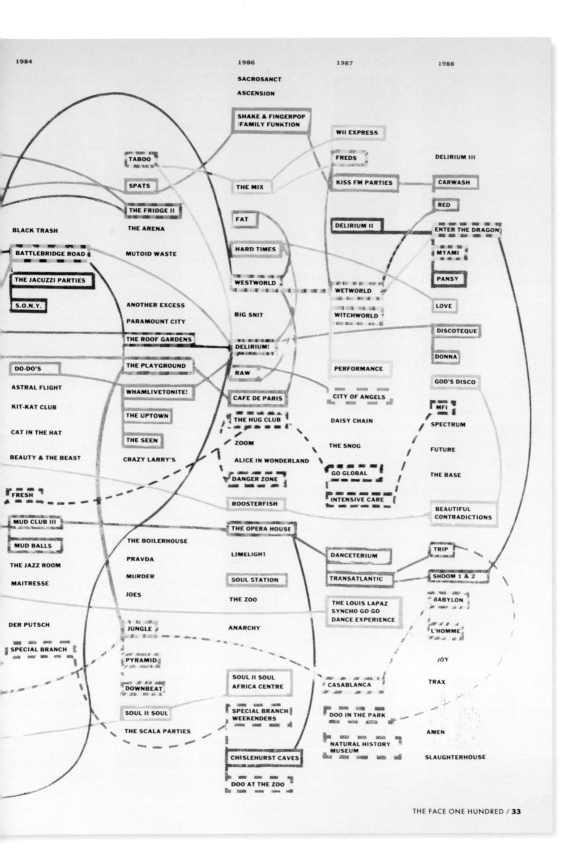

1984   1986   1987   1988

SACROSANCT

ASCENSION

SHAKE & FINGERPOP
/FAMILY FUNKTION

WII EXPRESS

TABOO   FREDS   DELIRIUM III

SPATS   THE MIX   KISS FM PARTIES   CARWASH

THE FRIDGE II   BED

THE ARENA   FAT   DELIRIUM II   ENTER THE DRAGON

BLACK TRASH   HARD TIMES   MYAMI

BATTLEBRIDGE ROAD   MUTOID WASTE   PANSY

THE JACUZZI PARTIES   WESTWORLD   WETWORLD   LOVE

S.O.N.Y.   ANOTHER EXCESS   WITCHWORLD

PARAMOUNT CITY   BIG SNIT   DISCOTEQUE

THE ROOF GARDENS   DELIRIUM!   DONNA

DO-DO'S   THE PLAYGROUND   RAW   PERFORMANCE   GOD'S DISCO

ASTRAL FLIGHT   WHAMLIVETONITE!   CAFE DE PARIS   CITY OF ANGELS   MFI

KIT-KAT CLUB   THE UPTOWN   THE HUG CLUB   DAISY CHAIN   SPECTRUM

CAT IN THE HAT   THE SEEN   ZOOM   THE SNOG   FUTURE

BEAUTY & THE BEAST   CRAZY LARRY'S   ALICE IN WONDERLAND   GO GLOBAL   THE BASE

FRESH   DANGER ZONE   INTENSIVE CARE

ROOSTERFISH   BEAUTIFUL
CONTRADICTIONS

MUD CLUB III   THE OPERA HOUSE

MUD BALLS   THE BOILERHOUSE   LIMELIGHT   DANCETERIUM   TRIP

THE JAZZ ROOM   PRAVDA   SHOOM 1 & 2

MAITRESSE   MURDER   SOUL STATION   TRANSATLANTIC

JOES   THE ZOO   BABYLON

THE LOUIS LAPAZ
SYNCHO GO GO
DANCE EXPERIENCE

DER PUTSCH   JUNGLE   ANARCHY   L'HOMME

SPECIAL BRANCH

PYRAMID   JOY

SOUL II SOUL
DOWNBEAT   AFRICA CENTRE   CASABLANCA   TRAX

SOUL II SOUL   SPECIAL BRANCH
WEEKENDERS   DOO IN THE PARK   AMEN

THE SCALA PARTIES   NATURAL HISTORY
MUSEUM

CHISLEHURST CAVES   SLAUGHTERHOUSE

DOO AT THE ZOO

Ethnomusicologist at Oxford University Martin Stokes also makes the case that music is laden with social meanings, 'largely because it provides means by which people recognize identities and places and the boundaries which separate them'. [8] In this respect London clubs in the 1980s provided a safe environment in which young people could mix with those with similar tastes. Fashion designer Stevie Stewart noted that 'each group of people, whether they were fashion designers, musicians or dancers, filmmakers or whatever, living together, going out together and at the same clubs ... had a passion then for creating something new ... that was almost infectious'. [9] Former stylist Dean Ricketts furthered this sentiment by observing how the relevance of London clubs was amplified by the influx of participants from outside the capital, all looking for somewhere that would accept their individuality and creativity. [10]

Commenting on London's clubs, journalist Robert Elms observed that, 'styles come and hold the beat for a while, usually going on to establish a permanent specialist nightclub audience, or else they go mainstream and become part of the fabric of British pop'. [11] Sociological observers Dick Hebdige and Ted Polhemus have also articulated the ways in which subcultural identity can be watered down following its adoption by the mainstream. [12]

The club model of Steve Strange and Rusty Egan was an example of increased specialisation within London's club scene. They would take over a venue for one night and create a weekly 'event' where the host, the DJ, the music and the crowd were collectively as important as the actual venue, a development that was replicated throughout the 1980s. Spandau Ballet's manager, Steve Dagger, noted that these nights were 'clubs run for kids by kids without feeling we were being ripped off'. [13] For DJ Jeffrey Hinton the specific site of the venue, be it a central London club attempting to fill a quiet night, or a disused warehouse for which the keys were made available, was important as 'you would find somewhere and then do something with it, rather than the other way round ... It was always to do with the actual place'. [14] The role of the host and door gatekeeper, and their idiosyncratic entry policy, was critical, both in setting the mood of the club and ensuring that those granted admission conformed to the particular ideology or dress code, so bestowing a particular subcultural capital upon the clientele. [15] Similarly, the DJ was 'responsible for the creation of a musical space, a space formed according to the expectations of the crowd and the specific kinds of DJ practices in place'. [16]

The connection between London clubs, music and fashion was furthered through collaborative events such as the 1981 New York trip to promote Spandau Ballet, the 'house band' at Blitz (23). Accompanied by their clubland friends – photographer, graphic designer and DJ Graham Smith, journalist Robert Elms and their manager Steve Dagger – Spandau Ballet played at New York nightclubs dressed by Jon Baker, Simon Withers and Melissa Caplan. Alongside, and as part of the 'roadshow', designers Caplan, Baker and Sullivan, together with Robin Archer, Paul Wynters and Demob, presented catwalk shows of their collections in the same New York venues. When McLaren and Westwood launched their *Pirates* collection in 1981, as well as holding a commercial fashion show at Olympia, they staged a show at Planets in Piccadilly, the nightclub run by one of the key faces of the London club scene, former punk Philip Sallon, and where (Boy) George O'Dowd was DJ. Similarly, to promote the new Axiom shop in Covent Garden in September 1981, a fashion show was held at Steve Strange's new Club for Heroes in Baker Street (24), and the following April, Strange took a group of designers (including Caplan, Linard, Robinson, PX, Dealey and Anthony Price) to Paris for a fashion show at the landmark nightclub Le Palace to launch his band Visage's second album, *The Anvil*. [17]

22 →
*Designer and lead
singer of Blue Rondo
à la Turk, Chris Sullivan
at Maestro club in
Glasgow, November
1981. Photograph by
David Johnson*

23 ↓
*Modern Classics
designs, worn by
Spandau Ballet at
the Ritz Hotel,
London, 1980.
Photograph by
Virginia Tubett*

In 1987 the fashion brand BOY (founded in 1977 by Stephane Raynor and now experiencing an international reputation with its recognizable print logo on clothes worn by Boy George and the Pet Shop Boys) held a catwalk show at Sallon's then notorious Mud Club at Busby's in Charing Cross Road. Thus London's cutting-edge young designers and musicians were being promoted within the clubbing environments in which they were thriving, as well as being exported outside London through such 'performances'. At the same time, the national and international press were reporting on both the innovative fashion and the unique style of nightclubs springing out of the capital.

In September 1982, the style magazine *The Face* described a shift in London's clubland away from the exaggerated, exotic styles that had been prevalent at the beginning of the decade towards a more 'functional' style of dress amongst both male and female clubbers (25). It also observed a 'hardening of attitudes in music and fashion' that reflected (rather than reacted against) the economic conditions of Thatcherite Britain with its massive unemployment, privatization of industry and the Falklands War: 'Ubiquitous Levi's worn into holes, sweatshirts serving their purpose and losing their sleeves, leather dominating everything ... big boots and no socks and espadrilles ... T-shirts ripped and torn'. [18] The 'Hard Times' look coincided with a revival of rockabilly style – in clothing, as sold at Jay Strongman's Kensington Market shop Rock-A-Cha and at Johnsons in Kensington Market and on the King's Road (26) [19]; and in music, played as part of an eclectic mix at various influential clubs.

24 ↓
Axiom fashion show at Club for Heroes, 1981. Photograph by David Johnson

At Gaz's Rockin' Blues at Gossips on Dean Street, rockabilly was played alongside reggae, ska, and rhythm and blues, and at Le Beat Route in Greek Street, alongside 'a mix of the sweetest soul of the seventies and the latest in radical funk'.[20] Dirtbox, cited by Elms as the Hard Times club, moved between various locations across London including disused warehouses, and as such was at the forefront of a trend that was to sweep through London's nightlife in the latter part of the decade: the acid house party and the subsequent explosion of rave culture (34).

The 'ripped up and torn' aspect of Hard Times style was also reflected in the look of new musical acts coming out of London's clubland, such as JoBoxers, with their depression era styling, and Haysi Fantayzee, with their mixture of 'African print and Dickensian and Tom Sawyer and Rasta'.[21] Fashion designers, too, were exploring a seemingly dishevelled look. Sue Clowes, who had dressed Boy George and his band Culture Club in her T-shirts, shirts and trousers in cross-cultural and religion-inspired prints (27), produced a 'hobo' collection in muted colours printed with 'the symbols that tramps used to scratch on trees or barns'.[22] McLaren and Westwood's 1982 *Buffalo* collection and the subsequent 1983 *Punkature* collection also featured oversized, distressed, mismatched and layered garments that were presented in a seemingly thrown-together mix of historic and multicultural influences. This mixing of influences and utilizing of found materials was employed by designers Christopher Nemeth and Judy Blame (who also ran Cha Chas at Heaven with hairdresser Scarlett). At London clubs Nemeth met like-minded creative individuals including shoe designer John Moore, knitwear designer Richard Torry, furniture design duo Frick and Frack, and jeweller Blame with whom he set up the collective The House of Beauty and Culture.

25 ↓
'Hard Times',
The Face, no. 29,
September 1982

26 ↘
Shop manager
Johnny 'Mono'
Graham outside
Johnsons, King's
Road, London, 1981.
Photograph by Ted
Polhemus

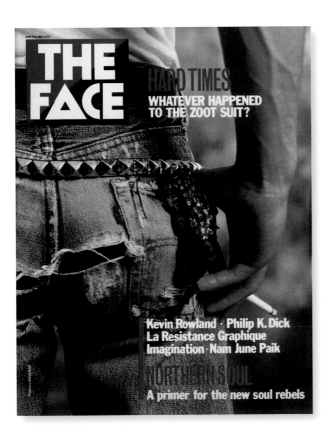

27 ↑
Sue Clowes designs,
worn by Culture
Club, 1981.
Photograph by
Clive Dixon

28 →
Christopher Nemeth
suit and accessories
in window of Bazaar,
South Molton Street,
London, 1986.
Photograph by
Nicola Townsin

Nemeth's clothes were made of 'a patchwork of fabrics': un-dyed hessian sacking and calico juxtaposed with woollen suiting, with rope fastenings and top stitching as decorative detail (28). [23] Blame, who created his jewellery and decorated accessories from salvaged objects, a technique he had developed for creating his own clothes, also worked with the stylist Ray Petri, whose Buffalo collective created visual identities across fashion and music that uniquely combined sportswear, military clothes, classic tailoring and unusual accessories. Petri, well-known in London's clubland, drew many of his ideas from those around him, creating a symbiotic relationship of influences between the nightclubs and style magazines, such as *The Face*, *i-D* and *Arena*. A review in *i-D* magazine of the new Black Market night, held on Fridays at the Wag Club (opened by Sullivan and Antenna hairdresser Ollie O'Donnell in October 1982), described 'the ever-present Petriboys in their MA1s, 501s and D.M.'s who come to hear "rare grooves" [and] the sparse kinetic rhythms of Chicago "House" music'. This highlighted the garments, along with head-to-foot knits, that had become a uniform of mid-1980s London clubbing (29, 30). [24]

This is not to say that all personal creativity had left the city's clubland. In 1987, *i-D* noted that when 'garments like denim and MA-1 flying jackets became too popular, an artistic burst of customizing soon turns them from a uniform back into a unique outfit' (31). [25] Many of London's clubs still promoted the idea of unique style in their door policy to attract a clientele of like-minded people. They were often run by those who frequented the late 70s/early 80s nights: Philip Sallon ran Planets and later the Mud Club with DJ Tasty Tim; Stephen Linard ran Total Fashion Victim at the Wag with DJs Princess Julia and Jeffrey Hinton; Denzil and milliner Paul Bernstock co-ran White Trash in Piccadilly; Princess Julia also hosted the gay night – Daisy Chain – at The Fridge in Brixton; [26] and Leigh Bowery, who had moved to London from Australia to attend the clubs he had read about, hosted Taboo at Maximus in Leicester Square (32).

Developing his exaggerated personal style by using clubs as catwalks, as well as briefly selling his designs at a stall in Kensington Market with fellow clubber and fashion designer Rachel Auburn, Bowery took the unconventional, the unfashionable and the offensive to create something new and unique. At Taboo, so-called because 'there is nothing you can't do there', Bowery quickly became the ringmaster of a carnivalesque nightspot, where parodying the norms of everyday life (and to an extent 'fashion') was encouraged (33). [27] Taboo's extreme eclecticism was reflected in DJ Hinton's musical approach of 'mixing a lot of things up. So I'd have Italo music and punk music and pop music, TV theme music and videos and sound effects'. [28] Being close friends with Bowery and Hinton (using them as model and DJ respectively at their fashion shows), fashion designers Bodymap were frequent attendants at Taboo, along with other friends/collaborators such as choreographer Michael Clark, and filmmakers John Maybury and Cerith Wyn Evans. By intermingling in what Bodymap's David Holah described as 'our own little fashion bubble', [29] a collective creative energy emerged. Stevie Stewart, Holah's partner at Bodymap, stated that this mixing and matching, or 'bricolage', was reflected in the titles and themes of their collections, such as *Cat in the Hat takes a Rumble with a Techno Fish*, which pulled together elements of Dr Seuss's surreal cartoon comedy, black-and-white graphics, bright colours and 1980s American 'bratpack' films, and ended up 'like a snowball rolling down and gathering momentum and influences along the way'. [30] Taboo closed after 18 months following a story in the tabloid newspaper *Mail on Sunday* that reported, 'Taboo's distinctive drug is ecstasy' and emphasized the hedonistic behaviour of the clientele. [31] In his 1998 exploration of rave culture, journalist Matthew Collin noted that Taboo was one of the earliest Ecstasy clubs in London, and as such acted as a precursor to the later Ecstasy-fuelled acid house parties. [32] In this respect Taboo, and the other clubs that attracted the same crowd, such as Daisy Chain, White Trash and the Mud Club, marked the clubbing intersection between the 'Blitz Kids' and acid house raves.

29 ↑
Outside the Wag Club, London, 1987. Photograph by David Swindells

30 ↗
Striped top and leggings, in the style of Bodymap, at the Astoria, London, 1987. Photograph by David Swindells

31 →
Girl in decorated MA-1 jacket at the Mud Club, London, 1984. Photograph by Derek Ridgers

32 →
*Leigh Bowery and
Gerlinde Costiff at
Taboo, London, 1985.
Collection of
Michael Costiff*

33 ↘
*Clubbers including
Princess Julia,
Scarlett, Nicola
Bateman, Malcolm
Duffy, Stephen
Brennon, Lana Pellay
and Mark Lawrence
at Taboo, London,
1985. Photograph
by Mr Hartnett*

Of course, while many London nightclubs in the mid-1980s shared this pivotal position between fashion (or style) and music, not all were about the excesses of dressing up to outrage. Barrie K. Sharpe, the founder of clothes shop Duffer of St George, was also DJ at the Wag and the Cat in the Hat Club, which opened in 1985 in London's Leicester Square. Duffer initially sold Liberto jeans, Sta-Prest trousers, Duffer's own brand suede-trimmed 70s-style cardigans; and caps, which Sharpe wore backwards while DJ-ing (35). Then in 1987 Duffer began to sell platform shoes and flares, stylistically reflecting the interest in 70s funk and 'rare-groove' soul music, which Sharpe and his partner Lascelles had brought to club-goers' attention at the Wag and the Cat in the Hat Club. London collective Soul II Soul operated in a similar way to Sharpe, running a clothes shop by day and a club by night: 'We're not just DJs, we're not just composers of music,' founder Jazzie B told *i-D* in 1989 (36). 'We want to show fashion collections eventually and elevate the fashion of Soul II Soul to the same heights as the music'. [33] Growing out of the Jah Rico reggae-based sound system in north London in the mid-1970s, Jazzie B and partner Daddae progressed from staging blues dances and warehouse parties to holding the Family Funktion nights at various London locations with other up-and-coming DJs such as Judge Jules, to the Africa Centre nights in Covent Garden, and Soul II Soul club nights at The Fridge. Jazzie B recalled that part of the success of Soul II Soul was that they 'grew up the same as these kids. We led the same lives – raving, on the street'. [34] His sentiments reflect those of many who created club nights in London throughout the 1980s. The Soul II Soul shop in Camden High Street sold sportswear-dominated clothes designed by Nicoli Bean, much of which incorporated the Funki Dred logo originally designed by Derek Yates for DJs' T-shirts, and which reflected 'the roots of their reggae culture and style of the urban dance scene'. [35]

Jazzie B's experience of DJ-ing at warehouse parties ties the development of this particular set of club nights to a broader club development in London. In his reminiscence for djhistory.com, he recalls playing at 'rockabilly fashion parties' and other fashion-related parties, where he 'played mainly electro. Man Parrish and few boogie-down Bronx and all them tunes'. This marked the arrival of American electronic, house and hip hop music, which was increasingly played at clubs and parties throughout the city (37). [36] One-nighters at established licensed venues, such as Gossips and the Wag in Soho, ran alongside one-off parties at warehouses and underused buildings, such as Dirtbox, and Circus hosted by DJs Hinton and Jeremy Healy, where new imports were mixed with eclectic personal taste in a variety of musical genres. The Wag as a venue was, as London tailor Mark Powell recalled, the 'first club from our scene that ran seven nights ... Every night was so different but somehow linked'. [37]

35 ↗
Barrie K. Sharpe, record sleeve for 'Love or Nothing' by Diana Brown and Barrie K. Sharpe. On the cover of this single Brown is wearing the suede trimmed cardigan and Sharpe is wearing his trademark knitted skull cap, both sold at Sharpe's shop, Duffer of St George.

36 →
Jazzie B in Soul II Soul, c.1988. Photograph by David Swindells

Imported house music from Chicago and Detroit had initially been popularized at clubs with a predominantly gay clientele, such as Delirium, Pyramid at Heaven and the Mud Club, where it was played by DJs such as Colin Favour and Mark Moore. Following the summer of 1987, a number of DJs began to recreate the sound and atmosphere of the Ecstasy-fuelled Ibiza dance clubs. That November, Danny Rampling hosted Shoom night at a gym in Southwark, south London, where the invitation read: 'Sensation Seekers, let the music take you to the top' (38). [38] Other nights followed, such as Confusion, the Trip, Love at the Wag and Paul Oakenfold's Spectrum at Heaven, where the 'loved up', euphoric feeling created by the combination of dance music and drugs (MDMA/Ecstasy) created an atmosphere in which 'inhibitions were totally gone. People used to start painting each other Day-Glo [and] reverting back to a childlike way'.[39] The 'friendly and fun' atmosphere, in which clubbers could 'totally relax and freak out', began to be reflected in the styles of clothing worn. [40] The dressed-up aesthetic of earlier clubs, like Taboo, was replaced by a much more casual combination: '... ponchos, dungarees, and loose T-shirts bearing yellow Smiley motif are considered stylish,' reported Sheryl Garrett in *The Face* in June 1988. [41] DJ Terry Farley noted that despite the seeming uniformity, there was still attention to detail amongst many of the clubbers: 'I hear people say that it didn't matter what you wore in those days – that's absolute bollocks. You might have been wearing dungarees, but it had to be the right dungarees, and you knew that they were'. [42] As the acid house club scene grew and became increasingly notorious, its style in music and fashion was disseminated across the country through popular media, such as BBC TV's *Top of the Pops* and tabloid newspaper the *Sun*'s 'acid house fashion guide', and their own Smiley T-shirt. It was time for the fashionable to move on.

London's clubs in the 1980s acted as a site for the confluence of music and fashion, from the plethora of exaggerated, exotic styles and early electronic music favoured by the Blitz Kids, through the distressed styles of Hard Times, to the eclectic mixing of music and individual expression of Taboo, to the dance-influenced comfort of acid house and beyond. This interaction was the result of the creative energy generated by the nightclubbing scene, whose influence spread still further to embrace almost every aspect of British cultural life – not solely music and fashion but also design, journalism, hairdressing, photography, dance and performance art – in the decades that followed.

—

Thanks go to Jeffrey Hinton, David Holah, Lloyd Johnson, Giselle La Pompe Moore, Kasia Maciejowska, Leigh Odimah, Dean Ricketts and Stevie Stewart for their time, thoughts and assistance on this essay.

37 ↖
Clubbers wearing hip hop and cycling gear at UK Fresh Hip Hop event, Wembley, London, 1986. Photograph by Mr Hartnett

38 ←
Clubbing at original acid house club, Shoom, London, 1988. Photograph by David Swindells

Daniel Milford-Cottam

The shoemaker Patrick Cox graduated from Cordwainer's in 1985 and became known for his bold footwear which included built-up platforms and unusual details, such as drawstrings on soft suede shoes. These elegant black leather slingbacks literally lock onto their wearer by means of a functioning padlock. This gives an already seductive pair of shoes an unexpected sexual frisson, suggesting that only the key bearer can release the wearer from her heels. More unexpected metalwork appears on Red or Dead's men's lace-ups, which feature a working wristwatch strapped over the lacing. The Red or Dead clothing label, founded in 1982 by Wayne Hemingway, began its footwear range in 1986. In 1987 the 'Watch' shoe was its most sought-after design.

PATRICK COX/ RED OR DEAD

39
Patrick Cox, women's 'Padlock'
slingback shoes, 1989.
V&A: T.365&A−1990
Red or Dead, men's 'Watch' shoes,
Summer 1988.
V&A: T.115&A−1989

Judy Blame's anarchic, unique and unisex statement jewellery was often used by stylists for photo shoots for *i-D* magazine. This image, styled to suggest a Victorian mudlark scavenging the banks of the Thames, features a necktie-cum-necklace, studded with tarnished buttons and scrap metal fragments. In addition to scrap metal, Blame comfortably incorporated rubber, string, shells, feathers, broken frames, kitchen utensils, and even carpet into his huge necklaces, brooches and rings. His uncompromising designs reveal the aesthetic merit of items that might otherwise have been written off as worthless rubbish. This approach was particularly potent at a time when many disaffected young people in the early 1980s were faced with high unemployment and lack of prospects. Blame worked closely with Leigh Bowery and created pieces for musicians including Duran Duran, The Transmitters and Boy George. He also worked as a stylist to the singer Neneh Cherry.

JUDY BLAME

40
Judy Blame, Father Thames, 1981.
Photograph by Robyn Beeche

Part 02

LONDON CALLING

Designer Fashion in 1980s London / Sonnet Stanfill

The English have an advantage over the French and the Italians: they don't get bogged down with notions of good or bad taste. [1]

Thirty-five years ago, the V&A inaugurated the 1980s with a ground-breaking project, the *British Fashion Designers 1979 Exhibition*. Showcasing 25 individual designer collections from the Autumn/Winter 1979 season, it was the museum's first exhibition devoted exclusively to contemporary British fashion.

The project launched at Simpson (Piccadilly) Limited in February 1979, with a black tie, champagne reception, and then opened at the Museum two months later (41). [2] The exhibition's participants, including Murray Arbeid, Wendy Dagworthy and Michiko Koshino, would help set the pace of London designer fashion throughout the following decade (42). Not only did the *British Fashion Designers 1979 Exhibition* mark a turning point in the V&A's dynamic engagement with home-grown fashion; it also called attention to the breadth and tenor of London's higher-end fashion talent, and the design issues that would preoccupy its protagonists.

One such preoccupation of London's fashion designers was playing with proportion. Moving away from the lean lines of 1970s style, a taste for layered looks developed, along with an openness to distortion of the natural form. In response, many designers, like Japan-born, London-based Michiko Koshino, continually engaged in enlarging, enveloping or constricting the body's silhouette.

41 ↓
Invitation for opening party, British Fashion Designers 1979 Exhibition, printed cotton.
V&A archives

The Directors of Simpson (Piccadilly) Limited request the pleasure of your company at the British Fashion Designers 1979 Exhibition presented by Barbara Griggs to be held at Simpson (Piccadilly) Ltd London W1 on Monday 26th February 1979.

RSVP Social Secretary
Black tie
Champagne 7.00 pm
Buffet Supper
Entrance Jermyn Street

42 ↓
*View of British
Fashion Designers
1979 Exhibition,
installed at the V&A,
including Michiko
Koshino ensemble.
V&A archives*

WENDY DAGWORTHY

PLEASE
DO NOT
TOUCH

PLEASE
DO NOT
TOUCH

PLEASE
DO NOT
TOUCH

43 ←
*Michiko Koshino ensemble,
shown in <u>British Fashion
Designers 1979 Exhibition,</u>
Autumn/Winter 1979 collection.
V&A: T.265-270&A–1980.
Given by the designer*

44 ↓
*Gerlinde Costiff wearing
Malcom McLaren and
Vivienne Westwood <u>Buffalo</u>
collection ensemble, Autumn/
Winter 1982. Worn at the
Easter Parade, Battersea
Park, London, April 1983.
Collection of Michael Costiff*

Koshino's Autumn/Winter 1979 collection initiated a series of attempts to alter the female form, first through padded clothing, then through the inflatable plastic garments with which she experimented more explicitly with amplification of body shape (43). During the 1980s (and beyond) Vivienne Westwood experimented relentlessly with bodily proportions. From the swathes of layered printed cotton Malcolm McLaren and she used for the *Pirate* collection of Autumn/Winter 1981, to her bulbous skirts of Spring/Summer 1985's *Mini Crini* and the continuous reworking of her signature restrictive corsets, Westwood's designs redefined the decade's corporeal contours. Most notably, the dishevelled volume of the *Buffalo* collection (also called *Nostalgia of Mud*) of Autumn/Winter 1982 completely disguised the wearer's form by layering sheepskin jackets over three-quarter length wool skirts augmented by bulky petticoats (44). One long-time client described their woollen comfort as, 'fantastic for New York winters'. [3]

45 ↓
*John Galliano,
ensemble from his
Les Incroyables
graduation collection.
Harpers & Queen,
December 1984.
Photograph by Rudi
Molacek*

46 ↘
*John Galliano,
ensemble from
Spring/Summer
1986 collection.
Harpers & Queen,
March 1986.
Photograph by
Mario Testino*

47 →
*Murray Arbeid, black
velvet evening dress
with red taffeta
skirt, 1986.
V&A: T.672–1996*

Furthering this vogue for designing with layered textiles, John Galliano's 1984 collection, with which he graduated from St Martin's School of Art, celebrated multiple, luxurious fabrics capaciously cut with historic proportions in mind (45). *Harpers & Queen* praised Galliano's 'Gracious lengths of organdie and brocade' and the 'vertical freedom' of his designs, suggestive of the eighteenth century. [4] Subsequent Galliano collections gambled further with shape and silhouette. His designs for Spring/Summer 1986 noticeably elongated the body and also amplified its form. A dress of honeycomb-knitted jersey, for example, featured pannier-like folds of excess fabric over the hips, while oversized cuffs exaggerated the line of the arm (46). Even conventional eveningwear, like the formal gowns crafted by Murray Arbeid, showed signs of experimentation with volume and proportion, leading to styles like the uneven hemline (47).

Reversing the trend for voluminous shapes of the early 1980s, transformative advances in textile technology, which allowed almost any material to have stretchable fibres woven into it, encouraged a closely fitted look towards the end of the decade. Many British designers embraced the streamlining properties of these new fabrics. Katharine Hamnett praised them as, 'the ultimate in figure revealing, both sexy and practical' and 'equally great for city dressing or mountain climbing'. [5] The slick city chic of the late 1980s was epitomized by these body-hugging fashions, created with the aerobicized form in mind (48).

48 ↓
Body-conscious dressing in 1980s Britain: Katharine Hamnett cotton Lycra leggings, Giorgio Sant'Angelo Spandex tube and Union leather jacket. Vogue, July 1987. Photograph by Jim Varriale

49 ↘
Ensemble with exotic references, i-D, no. 24, April 1985. Styled by Rifat Ozbek, photograph by Johnny Rozsa

The unforgiving nature of stretch fibres requires a slim, youthful figure, as British *Vogue* cautioned its readers in the July 1987 issue: 'Keeping your body supple and strong is still more essential now every muscle of it is on show'. The magazine continued:

Stretch is fashion's dynamic force, a challenge for designer and wearer alike. A new way of flexing every fabric from silk satin to wool crepe. It's the sexiest dressing yet, hiding the body and at the same time, showing its every movement, sounding every curve of bosom and waistline, hips and thighs.

In addition to experimenting with silhouettes and with new textile technologies, designers in 1980s London were quick to explore new fabric designs. Colour and pattern, including those for knitwear, underwent dramatic style changes. Though the aesthetic was constantly shifting, there was always room for rich colour, exotic references and bold pattern. During this decade, London-based designers often referenced non-Western traditions through their use of fabric. After concluding his studies at Saint Martin's School of Art in 1976, Rifat Ozbek's work as a stylist and a designer celebrated a multicultural exoticism. His choice of textiles, surface ornament and accessories suggested cultural wanderings (49). One report, neatly summarizing his talent, stated, 'Rifat Ozbek travels through his native Middle East for inspiration. The Turkish-born designer takes a sleek,

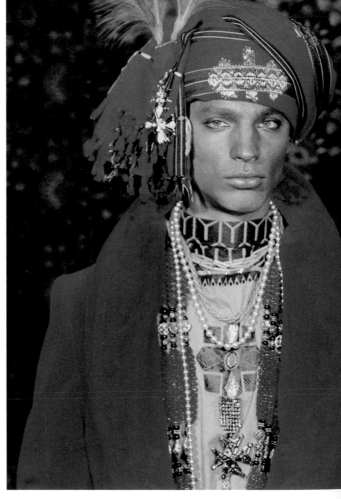

50 ↓
Rifat Ozbek, white silk organza shirt, silk moiré cummerbund, crimson crepe pencil skirt with gold embroidered hem; turquoise fez by Philip Sommerville; Spring/Summer 1987 collection. Vogue, February 1987. Photograph by Neil Kirk

51 ↘
Crolla, metallic trousers, twisted into cornucopia headwear, Autumn/Winter 1985 collection. Harpers & Queen, October 1985. Photograph by Andrew Macpherson

sophisticated approach to the clothes of other cultures. He borrows djellaba stitching from Afghanistan, leopard prints and belts from Africa and the moon, stars and ikat fabrics from Tibet … All the clothes are shown with Turkish slippers' (50). [6] Scott Crolla also designed with rich fabrics, suggestive of non-Western locales (51). *The Face* described Crolla's look as, 'A perfect blend of adventurous tailoring and witty fabrics; fine cotton suits, shirts in African and Indian brocades, silk damask for pyjamas, dressing gowns and slippers.' [7]

While some London fashion designers sourced a seductive array of exotic textiles from varied suppliers, others commissioned fabrics from a formidably talented group of British print designers. Their craftsmanship helped to sustain this important British tradition. As one American press report enthused:

The fabric explosion takes its energy and style from the print designers who are pouring out of England's colleges — which many people consider the finest in the world … English textile designers, perhaps because of their excellent fine arts education, give their work a painterly, highly individualistic flavor rarely seen elsewhere. [8]

Influential practitioners included the well-established Zandra Rhodes, along with, among others, Timney Fowler, Victoria Richards and Georgina van Etzdorf. Some of the period's most striking prints were those designed by English Eccentrics, founded by Helen David (née Littman), a Camberwell and Saint Martin's trained print-maker, along with her sister Judy and their friend Claire Angel. A 1984 screen-printed fashion textile confirms their flair for the complex (53). This elaborate, discharge-dyed silk suggests a mosaic of broken china with motifs including architectural drawings and tile fragments. Another notable design collaboration was The Cloth, founded by a quartet of Royal College of Art printed textile graduates: David Band, Brian Bolger, Helen Manning and Fraser Taylor. This collective, who also turned their talents to interiors, book illustration and graphic design, created textiles for prominent London fashion designers such as Jean Muir, Paul Smith and Betty Jackson (52). Said Fraser Taylor, 'We don't consider ourselves clothing people. It's painting on fabric'. [9] *Newsweek* magazine concurred, stating, 'The Cloth, a design collective consisting of four 25-year-old graduates of the Royal College of Art, has become extremely popular for its bold expressionistic approach to fabric'.[10]

By harnessing the talents of textile designers fresh from art college, London's fashion designers not only satisfied the demand for stylish prints but also helped their fledgling fashion businesses meet delivery deadlines. Buying textiles from abroad meant taking a chance on late delivery. Recalled Wendy Dagworthy:

> **Production is every designer's nightmare. You order the fabric, and then after you've shown the collection and taken your orders, you book space at a small factory. But if the fabric arrives late, that results in cancellations. [11]**

Fashion journalist Sally Brampton detailed the London designer's dilemma:

> **While most of our top designers can find the quality of the fabric they require from British mills, they cannot find good colours, so they buy from Italy. The Italians, naturally, deliver to their own designers first, and in the pecking order which follows, Britain comes last. So when our designers are blamed for lack of professionalism in their late deliveries, it is more that their hands are tied by their own and the Italian textile industries. [12]**

For these reasons, Paul Smith's early textile choices for his self-described 'tailoring with a twist' were often British, usually sourced from London stock houses, where he could buy the fabrics literally off the shelf. Explaining the impossible quandary of a small designer's textile selection, he stated:

> **One of the things that designers suffered from then, but in fact still suffer from now, is the chicken and egg scenario: if you haven't got enough orders, you can't hit the minimum quantities you need to buy the fabric to have things made, and you haven't got any orders because you haven't got a collection. So which comes first? [13]**

While the careers of many influential textile designers were forged in the 1980s, British knitwear also thrived and new techniques, silhouettes and patterns were both celebrated and commercialized. Sandy Black, former knitwear designer and now professor at the London College of Fashion, has chronicled with elegance the development of the post-war knitting boom and the craft revival that followed. [14] This renewed interest in craft and an accompanying enthusiasm for the handmade propelled to prominence designers such as Bill Gibb and his collaborations with Kaffe Fassett. The work of Patricia Roberts, Artwork, Sarah Dallas and Kay Cosserat further fuelled the seemingly limitless international appetite for hand-knitted garments, which have remained an undisputed strength of British fashion production. And it was knitwear that became the key component of the new body-conscious wardrobe.

54 ↓
Bodymap's form-fitting, knitted designs. Harpers & Queen, September 1984. Photograph by Tony McGee

55 ↘
Joseph Tricot's richly patterned knitwear, Autumn/Winter 1988 collection. Blitz, March 1986. Photograph by Gill Campbell

LIVE-WIRE DEFINITION:
BODY MAP'S
HEALTHY OPPORTUNIST
STRIP SWEATS.
SPRUNG FROM THE STREETS,
SHARPENED IN THE CLUBS
TO THE FAST
DIGITAL ELECTRO-BEAT,
THE NEW GRAFFITI LEGS
(AS INTENSELY PULSED AS
VIDEO-SCRATCHED VISUALS)
ARE SHARPLY
RHYTHMICAL PRINT-OUTS

56 ↓
*Joseph Tricot, man's
red jumper with
tiger pattern,
c.1985.
V&A: T.90—2009.
Given by
Martin Kamer*

Bodymap, founded in 1982 by Stevie Stewart and David Holah, produced an exhilarating blend of form-fitting knits, layered stretch Lycra jersey and rhythmic print that presaged the new look to come (54). Their collections balanced irreverence and fashionable appeal with offbeat offerings such as boxy cropped jumpers, patterned stockings and tight-fitting, knitted shorts. As one fashion editorial noted, their inspiration had 'sprung from the streets, sharpened in the clubs'. [15] The designers gained further momentum through their collaborations from mid-decade with ground-breaking choreographer Michael Clark, whose commissions of Bodymap's costume designs produced visually arresting results. The duo's designs, with knitted garments as a constant component, were assured and potent symbols of innovative London fashion. As such, they were sold through the capital's upscale boutiques, including Joseph, the shop owned by designer and retailer Joseph Ettedgui, who offered a selection of designer fashion alongside his own eponymous lines. From the mid-1980s his Joseph Tricot knitwear label catered to the taste for oversized shapes and bold patterns, his chunky, abstracted Fair Isle patterns epitomizing the high end interpretation of the craze for hand-knitted garments (55, 56).

A concurrent development in 1980s knitwear was the overt appeal of highly decorative, whimsical designs, exemplified by the work of Beth Brett, who operated her London-based knitwear business from 1975 to 1990. Brett, like many knitwear designers, produced garments in the homes of outworkers; at the decade's peak she employed between 10 and 20 knitters. She would finish the designs herself and then sell them to leading British and American stores, including Liberty's, Joseph, Harrods, Saks Fifth Avenue and Neiman Marcus. This so-called 'fantasy knitwear' might include a mix of techniques from knitting and appliqué to leather detailing and beadwork, infinitely extending the possibilities of a knitted garment (57).

As with knitwear and printed textiles, fine tailoring is a part of Britain's fashion heritage. And for London-based designers in the 1980s it provided not only a source of inspiration but also a tradition to subvert. In fact, throughout the decade the tailored garment was continually referenced and frequently transformed. Such experiments helped Britain's tailoring techniques evolve, in both menswear and womenswear, by giving them fashionable appeal.

42 /
Beth Brett, jacket of
knitted gold-latticed
sleeves with leather
fringe, appliqué and
beadwork, c.1985.
V&A: T.79–2009.
Given by Herb
Goldschmidt in
memory of Beth Brett

58 ↓
**Paul Smith
sketchbook,
Autumn/Winter
1987 collection.
Collection of
Paul Smith**

Influenced by the softer fabrics of Italian tailoring and the deconstruction of the jacket, tailored clothing, across the fashion capitals, became less structured and more pliant. Paul Smith energized his suits and tailored wardrobes with bold colour and unexpected design features, such as drawstring waists and elasticated details (58). Like Smith, the esoteric designer and retailer Willy Brown toyed with tradition. Representing a more utilitarian version of tailored garments, Brown sold his designs through his Rivington Street shop. The ensembles often referenced work clothing and the uniform with functional snap fastenings, aprons, the drop-fronted construction of sailor's trousers and the use of army surplus fabrics. His clothes were a direct nod to industrial workwear, but with distinctive detailing (59). Former client Philip Hoare described Brown's mix of the traditional and the offbeat: 'My first purchase was a khaki suit with green collar detail and embroidered runes, in a Bavarian/Nordic style'. [16]

Some designers merged the exaggerated proportions of 1980s fashion with the tailored look. Alistair Blair, who also crafted elegant eveningwear, added stylish appeal to traditional garments with details such as oversized, padded shoulders (60). John Galliano transferred his experiments with silhouette and form to menswear, creating layered, asymmetrical deconstructions (61). Other designers, such as Graham Fraser and Richard Nott of Workers For Freedom, enlivened tailored clothing with appliqué or embroidery, the jacket or waistcoat becoming a canvas for bold surface decoration (62). Wrote one journalist of their Autumn/Winter 1988 designs, 'The collection was their best yet ... it included the designers' signature embroidered blouses with soft, ruffled collars, slim embroidered pants and Burmese-style suits with Neru [sic] jackets'. [17] In this way Workers For Freedom succeeded in making men's and women's clothing adventurous, without being outrageous.

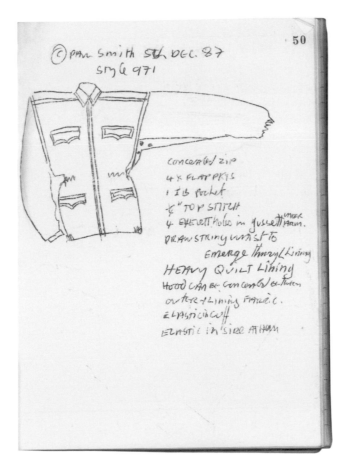

59 ↓
*Willy Brown, green
cotton suit with
Tyrolean details;
hand-painted cotton
dress. Both c.1980.
V&A: T.14:1–2–2012;
V&A: T. 19—2012.
Given by Philip Hoare*

60 ↘
*Alistair Blair,
ensemble from
Autumn/Winter
1986 collection.
Harpers & Queen,
October 1986*

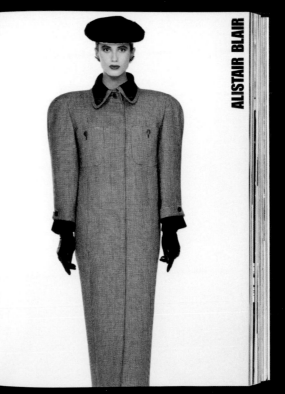

61 ↓
John Galliano, man's
suit with oversized
fit and asymmetrical
fastenings, 1985.
V&A: T.224:A–D–1989
and T.224&A–1990

62 ↘
Workers For
Freedom, men's
embroidered worsted
wool jacket, 1990.
V&A: T.446–1995

63↓
The Cloth (for Betty Jackson), advertisement for Saks Fifth Avenue, c.1984. Collection of Betty Jackson

64 ↘
Betty Jackson, ensemble from Autumn/Winter 1984 collection. Harpers & Queen, September 1984. Photograph by Tony McGee

The quieter side of 1980s fashion in the capital was represented by the work of a cluster of designers who created stylish wardrobes with simple components, eschewing elaborate surface decoration or applied ornament. Their offerings of less formal, loosely structured clothing, often made from British textiles, were designed to be worn from daytime into evening, with little more effort than changing accessories. Such clothes were usually sold through an international mix of department stores and independent boutiques. Betty Jackson composed pragmatic, chic ensembles, often placing considerable emphasis on the textiles themselves and mixing different prints within the same outfit. Jackson championed the textile designs of compatriots such as Timney Fowler and the design collective The Cloth (63), and was a vocal supporter of the freedom she enjoyed as a London-based designer, once stating, 'We don't have the same barriers as the French and Italians. We're not dictated to by anybody.' (64) [18]

BETTY JACKSON'S HIGH-LEVEL EXPOSURE: ELEMENTAL SEDUCTION IN VOLATILE BODY-SKIMMING CHIFFON, DRAMATISING WITH CATALYST COMBINATIONS – EVEN THE SHOE'S A SLIPPER

65 ↓
**Wendy Dagworthy,
ensemble from
Spring/Summer
1985 collection in
the window of Saks
5th Avenue, New
York, 1985.
Collection of
Wendy Dagworthy**

66 ↘
**Wendy Dagworthy,
printed cotton
ensemble from
Spring/Summer
1985 collection.
V&A: T.218 to E—1990.
Given by the designer**

An emphasis on textiles and informality also characterized Wendy Dagworthy's womenswear and menswear collections, sold to stores in Britain, the United States, Europe and South Africa throughout the decade (65). Her designs were made for modern urban lives – they had flexibility, with relaxed layers, such as leggings worn under skirts – but she would take delight in the small details, too. And while she often chose traditional British fabrics, such as Harris tweed, fine herringbone wools and knitted mohair (67), she might then feature multiple patterns within one outfit (66). In describing the design elements of her 1982 collection, Dagworthy said, 'I enjoyed doing this collection because it had features like sugar bag pockets, and I mixed traditional fabrics with things like ikats. An eclectic mix!' [19]

67 ↘
**Wendy Dagworthy,
wool suit with
mohair jumper,
Autumn/Winter
1984 collection.
V&A: T.25:1-2–2012,
T.26–2012. Given by
the designer**

68 ␣
Richmond/Cornejo,
printed cotton
dress, c.1984.
V&A: T.116–2012.
Given by
Dr Janice Hart

69 ↘
John Flett, Spring/
Summer 1986
collection. Harpers
& Queen, March
1986. Photograph by
Andrew Macpherson

Other proponents of the vogue for day-to-evening dressing included Saint Martin's-trained John Flett, whose imaginative, precisely constructed designs graced the catwalks of late 1980s London (69). The pared down designs of John Richmond and Maria Cornejo, who worked together for a number of years before pursuing successful individual careers, were eminently wearable but had an urban edge (68). A self-described designer of 'updated modern classics', Margaret Howell chose to move into womenswear from menswear with the advent of the 1980s. Maintaining an emphasis on British manufacturing and textiles, [20] she re-interpreted the schoolgirl gymslip, which became a signature look and personified her deft design economy (70).

The work of these London-based designers illustrates the deep reserves of creative talent that British fashion was able to drawn on in the 1980s. This was the decade when the city, through significant collective effort, secured its reputation as a source of internationally influential fashion. It is remarkable to consider how far, by the decade's end, the landscape had changed from what fashion journalist Kennedy Fraser described in an austere assessment, penned in 1977:

And high fashion must involve a kind of artistic elitism that may prick the conscience of its exponents — many of Britain's most determined new talents are the state-educated products of working-class backgrounds — in a welfare state whose commitment to egalitarian levelling-down extends from the government's policy of non-discriminatory education and health care to the fashion industry's traditional goal of cheap, if undistinguished, clothing for the masses. [21]

A measure of progress might be taken from an event staged less than ten years after Fraser's critique. In 1985, London hosted the glamorous, star-studded fundraiser Fashion Aid at the Royal Albert Hall. Aside from the visual feast provided by this catwalk show and music extravaganza, Fashion Aid was a self-conscious pronouncement of London's place in the fashion world. London fashion's key protagonists organised the event, which was held in a London landmark with many British designers participating. These included Anthony Price, Katharine Hamnett, the Emanuels, Zandra Rhodes, Bodymap and Scott Crolla, along with designers from other fashion capitals. Securing hundreds of thousands of pounds for charity, as a fundraising event Fashion Aid was successful. Televised around the world, as a PR exercise Fashion Aid was extraordinary, a vital vote of confidence in London's future as a fashion capital.

The end of the 1980s saw a palpable sense of optimism and assurance take hold. In the autumn of 1990, the British Fashion Council, the London Designer Collections and the British Clothing Industries Association announced plans to inaugurate a dedicated catwalk space at the Duke of York Headquarters on the King's Road, with the aim of making London, 'the centre for younger designers in Europe'. [22] Diana, Princess of Wales, presided over London Fashion Week's Spring 1990 collections at a high profile gala event again held at the Royal Albert Hall. Even fashion provocateur Vivienne Westwood acknowledged London's growing professionalism, stating, 'The gap is closing between street fashion and the fashion of the establishment.' [23] By the start of the next decade, London as a fashion city had evolved from scrappy contender to sophisticated, international protagonist. As one industry observer put it, 'Thanks to banks, investors and knowledgeable manufacturers, most of these young British designers are, at last, producing merchandise that can hold its own against what we've seen in Milan, Paris and the USA'. [24]

Daniel Milford-Cottam

By the 1980s spectacles had become a fashion accessory in their own right. Eyewear makers such as the London-based firm of Oliver Goldsmith took on the challenge of designing glasses that combined function with strong design, such as their distinctive 'Zig-Zag' frames of 1982. The striped detail, placed asymmetrically to curve around the eyes, was available in eight different colourways, and the frame itself came in four solid colours. Oliver Goldsmith's glamorous publicity photographs furthered the perception of spectacles as an important fashion accessory. Such clever promotions helped to make fashion-conscious eyewear widely available, with virtually all opticians today now offering a variety of designer frames for prescription use.

Accessory

OLIVER GOLDSMITH

71
Oliver Goldsmith, 'Zig-Zag' frames, 1982
Collection of Oliver Goldsmith

Roger Saul founded leather goods company Mulberry in 1971 to produce belts, bags and other accessories using traditional craftsmanship and saddle-making techniques. By the 1980s, Mulberry had become one of the largest British manufacturers and exporters of high end leather accessories. The maroon leather clutch bag and co-ordinating leather belt formed part of a ready-to-wear day outfit for Winter 1979. The bag is designed in a timeless style featuring Mulberry's tree logo embossed upon its leather flap, whilst the wide cinch belt is accented with blue embroidery and cutwork. They are versatile, well-made wardrobe staples, intended to have a long life. Mulberry today is still focused on classic forms and subtle detail for its quality handbags and other leather goods.

MULBERRY

72
*Mulberry, maroon leather clutch bag
and co-ordinating leather belt, Winter 1979.
V&A: T. 290–1980; T.294–1980*

Part 03

IRONY AND MYTH...

B O T T O M L E S S   W O N D E R

The silhouette to get is top-sided and bottomless. Raise a look to a peacock's crest, treat a torso with jackettes and silouettes, smooth to a fine line below the belt.

Derrieres are simple . . .

. . . take it all to the top

Photos Andrew Macpherson
Styling Caroline Baker
Hair-ups Simon Marsden for School
Make-ups Mary Greenwell
Model Nina Schultz

THE FACE

SEPTEMBER 1985 85p US $2.75

HOLIDAY BABYLON
NIGHTLIFE ON FANTASY ISLAND

HOLLYWOOD OR BUST
DREAMS OF THE SOHO TEENS

THE CULT/NORMAN MAILER
CAMEO/SIGUE SIGUE SPUTNIK
ARIF MARDIN/YUKIO MISHIMA

F A S H I O N N O T E S
● By Joe McKenna

As autumn approaches so too does the onslaught of fashion spreads depicting girls-as-boys. With the Olympics virtually upon us, we have hopefully seen the end of all those sub Bruce Weber models extolling the virtues of "plunging for purple", "racing for red" and, most irritating, "learning to shape the body and tone the muscles". Can't fashion editors ever present a **look** in a new and refreshing way? The current trend for girls bent on being homme-ward bound will soon be appearing — cropped hair for cropped hair, flat brogue for flat brogue — in countless magazine spreads. Fashion goes in cycles and this new winter trend sounds vaguely **Annie Hall without the perm** to me. If we really must ask "who wears the trousers?" in 1984, then can we at least try and answer it in a more interesting way? ● If you're more into a new pullover than an old legover, head for **Joseph Tricot** (Sloane St and South Molton St) where the look for this season is decidedly more **relaxed**. Sweaters and dresses are looser, roomier, **easier to wear**. The summer's famous hip-hugging tube skirt skirts the ankles and grows more voluminous, **balloon shaped** for winter. Colours are black, brown and grey through to emerald, purple and turquoise lambswool. Always brilliantly accessorised, Joseph has gone for Berrotock/Spiers **racey tartan motoring caps** with clashing tartan scarves. Belts have pockets, scarves attached bobble hats. The ascent of Joseph continues further this month with the opening of **Pour La Maison** at 16 Sloane St, housing amongst the household accessories the complete **Azzedine Alaïa, Crolla** and **Paul Smith**. And toward the end of the month the new **Kenzo** shop, modelled on its Paris parent opens at 27 Brook Street, London W1. ● **Bazooka** is a newly-formed design group (two ex-St Martins students plus one American) patronaged by the ubiquitous Joseph, but also on sale at Whistles and Browns. For winter a refreshing change: striped **school blazers** in reds, greens and navy. School ties, **mini gymskirts** and sweat fabric **skipants**. Watch out **Bodymap**! ● It was inevitable that the summer's most ripped-off garment would be **Katharine Hammett's** range of 'Peace' t-shirts. While the designer is delighted when the shirts are copied providing they bear a similarly sympathetic message (she's thrilled by the Soho shop selling **Save the GLC** shirts), she is outraged by Virgin's Megastore in Oxford Street who have bowlderised her 'Choose Life' slogan to less than witty 'Choose Wham!' ● So what if he does have a "spreading waistline, scruffy beard and wears a bandana", **Bruce Weber** is still the best and most influential fashion photographer in the

Menswear from Crolla, 28 Dover Street, London W1 ● Photography & styling by Sheila Rock ● Hair by Rene Gelston ● Makeup by Maggie Baker at Creative Workforce ● Model Julian at Marco Rasala

STOCKISTS FOR PAGES 44 - 47

'Designs by **Carol Graham, Julie Speechley, Sandra Devillo-Logati, Jane Howlett** and **Jackie Marsh** were all part of their recent final collections at Central Saint Martin's School of Art and Design. Enquiries about availability can be made through Bridget Jones, Head of the Fashion Department on 01-636 2426. **Midas**, Brompton Arcade, London SW1 and branches. **Whistles**, St Christopher's Pl, London W1 and branches. **Jones**, 129 and 71 King's Rd, London SW3. **Ameuld**, 52 Glendale Pl, London SW7. **Hobbs**, 84 Hampstead High St, London NW3, and 2 Marman's Square, Edinburgh. **Racquet**, 9 Malcolm Arcade, London. **Steet**, 1-3 Foubert's Arcade, Nottingham. **Browns**, 23-27 South Molton St, London W1. **Flandins**, 80 Floral St, London WC2. **Flip**, 125 Long Acre, London WC2. **Reiss**, 6 South Molton St, London W1. **Swanky Modes**, 46-48 Chamba Rd, London. **Robot**, 37 Floral St, London WC1. **Harvey Nichols**, Knightsbridge, London SW1. **Robot**, Floral St, London WC2 and 107 King's Rd, London SW3. **Margaret Howell**, 29

HE'S THE RISING STAR OF LONDON FASHION,
FROM TURKEY VIA AN ARCHITECTURE COURSE AT
LIVERPOOL UNIVERSITY. RIFAT OZBEK (LEFT)
PROFILED AND STYLED BY SARAJANE HOARE,
ILLUSTRATED BY TONY VIRAMONTES.

TALL, DARK AND HANDSOME, oozing with charm, 32-year-old Rifat Ozbek is the new designer darling of the London fashion scene. American buyers visiting his showroom during London's fashion week stare adoringly at him, side by side with his more chic young admirers. He provides clothes that appeal to the experienced and the ingenue. They are an invitation to be stylish without having to grapple with the mysterious pretentions and meanings of contemporaries like Galliano, Flett and Body Map.

The ballet photographs of George Platt-Lynes provide the inspiration for his new collection, while the music of Prokoviev and Copeland murmurs from the record player. Ozbek whips a series of garments in muted colours from a showroom rail and vanishes behind a screen to dress three models — who emerge minutes later resplendent as Margot Fonteyn look-a-likes, complete with eyeliner, red feathered hair bands, satin ballet shoes.

They swirl about on the creaking wooden floorboards wearing taupe and brown cashmere jackets, coats with velvet collars over stretch-wool leotards and high-waisted skirts. Others in stark black-crepe dresses with full, swirling skirts, knotted at the waist with a thick piece of rope, and more a tribute to the ballet clothes of Martha Graham.

Stripped of accessories and hanging on the show rails, his distinctly feminine clothes speak quietly of his simplistic approach to cut and design. Despite their European appeal, the clothes betray no trace of Ozbek's Turkish origins which he left behind aged 18 to study architecture at Liverpool University. After a brief stint at the Architectural Association in London he realised that "there was too much technical stuff in architecture like maths and physics that I couldn't get to grips with."

Like Balenciaga and Alaia who also trained in architecture, he channelled his talents into fashion design which he studied at St. Martin's School of Art. "I absolutely *loved* every minute of it. My degree show was a Highwayman's look — *beyond!*" he recalls laughingly, lounging back on a large crimson velvet sofa.

After St. Martin's he took a job as a designer at Monsoon which did not, he reckons, take him anywhere, but gave him a work permit. "I learnt about clothes mainly by looking at other people's clothes and seeing how they were cut and finished," he explains.

A Turkish associate has been backing his persistently good collections for the past two years. His first, shown at his parents' flat in London, was based on an African theme — but with European cuts — inspired by some Fortuny African-print furnishing fabric that he incorporated into the clothes. "I've gone from African to Beatnik to Italian Capri to ballet and I'm *not* going to tell you where I go next! I think designers should change, evolve and be different each season," he explains. "I don't want to do clothes for clothes' sake. Using different themes helps to give that certain edge of humour and amusement — it helps to give more of a style."

It is style that Ozbek searches for season after season. "I don't like it when people say that bad taste is good taste. That's rubbish; that's why one is called bad taste and one is called good taste."

His garments are an invitation to good taste.

44 THE FACE

With the exception of i-D there was nothing like The Face in a market comprised of inky music weeklies, posh glossy monthlies, and the teen mags. [1]

Writing in 2000, Nick Logan, the founding editor of *The Face*, succinctly describes the landscape of fashion and music magazines in Britain during the 1980s. Having edited an 'inky music weekly' and a 'teen mag' himself (*New Musical Express* and *Smash Hits*, respectively), Logan's main contribution to magazine culture came in May 1980 when, armed with the miniscule launch budget of £3,500, *The Face* hit British newsstands. As Logan recalls, 'there was a gap in the market ... for a glossy magazine that acknowledged the fashion end of music. Live photos ... so many of them were clichés. I didn't want to see Roger Daltrey's tonsils, his jacket was more interesting to me'. [2] Absorbing contemporary youth culture through a wide lens, *The Face* heralded the arrival of the 'style' magazine. Although the magazine's early bias was heavily tipped towards music, Logan notes, 'there had always been fashion in *The Face*', something that was 'implicit in the way we photographed and presented musicians'. [3] When presented more explicitly, fashion emerged through 'self-conscious set pieces' [4] by photographers such as Sheila Rock, whom Logan had brought to *The Face* from his time at *NME* and *Smash Hits*. Rock had cut her teeth photographing for the seminal punk fanzine, *Sniffin' Glue,* during the late 1970s. Reflecting the charged energy of punk music, fanzines such as this and *Ripped and Torn* channelled a DIY aesthetic through their photocopied pages, stapled bindings, collaged images, scrawled titles and strips of typewriter text (73). Although launching as an independent publisher, Logan's intention was for *The Face* to sell through major national newsagents. As he describes it, he didn't want a 'parish magazine' with a limited circulation, distributed through record shops and art bookshops, but rather, one that would compete with mainstream magazines on an equal footing. Logan wanted *The Face* to combine a sense of immediacy with the high-end production values of *Vogue* and *Tatler*. As he once stated, 'why should the devil have all the best tunes?' [5]

A magazine that perhaps adhered more faithfully to the tenets of the fanzine tradition was *i-D*. Launched by Terry Jones in August 1980, three months after *The Face, i-D* magazine adopted a radical agenda by showcasing street fashions and featuring non-professional models. Essentially a fashion fanzine, this 'exercise in social documentation' [6] evolved into a magazine that, alongside *The Face*, was considered a definitive 'style bible' of the 1980s. Before *i-D*, Terry Jones had spent much of his career working for the aforementioned 'posh glossy monthlies', serving as art director at *Vanity Fair* and British *Vogue*. At *Vogue*, Jones employed photographers who could challenge the magazine's 'manicured image'. [7] While the style at American *Vogue* was 'hard-edged', here Jones wanted 'more flesh and blood ... more soul and more energy', seeking the realism of documentary photography. Jones recalls that, despite the standard practice at *Vogue* to retouch every flaw in a photograph, 'retouching the creases out of a model's trouser leg seemed to kill an image rather than give it life'. [8] In 1976, conscious of the raw image-making to be found within fanzines, Jones set out to document the punk fashions of London's King's Road. Hoping to run the photographs as a *Vogue* fashion story, Jones asked Steve Johnston, a young photography student from Carlisle, to make simple head-to-toe portraits, utilizing a blank piece of wall as a stark backdrop. Johnston stopped people at this same spot over a period of three months, producing 'straight-up' photographs inspired by Irving Penn's studio portraits and August Sander's photo-classifications of German workers. Struggling to gain approval to print the images in *Vogue*, Jones published the photographs in 1978 as an independent project, *Not Another Punk Book!* Outlining the potential of punk and other street styles to

challenge the orthodoxies of commercial fashion magazines, Jones used the book to express his frustrations with the conservative attitudes at *Vogue*: 'Punk happened on the street, not in the pages of a fashion magazine, and the kids have a hard realism in refusing to be beguiled by glossy images and paternalistic hand-outs of style and culture.' [9] One of Jones's colleagues at *Vogue* was Caroline Baker, a stylist who during the 1960s and 1970s had made her name at *Nova*, Britain's first true 'street fashion' magazine. Baker admits that she didn't last long at *Vogue* because she was 'dismissed as a punk' and her stories were 'too street-wise for the upper-class snobbish attitudes' that dominated the magazine at the time. Recognizing a kindred spirit in Jones, Baker became a regular contributor to *i-D*. She recalls that Jones always went 'below the surface of dress', creating a space where she was 'encouraged to respond to fashion movements, without any editorial constraints … a great environment to work in, and one I have never encountered anywhere else in my career as a fashion editor.' [10] Jones asked Johnston to continue with his 'straight-up' street portraits, which defined the early look of *i-D*. These issues were produced in a landscape A4 format, thus suggesting the width of a street populated with people and their bespoke, contrasting styles (74).

Although Steve Johnston's straight-ups were influenced by the work of early twentieth-century photographers such as Sander and Penn, their neutral 'gaze' reflects broader traditions of fashion design in-house documentation. Capturing a season's collection through illustration or photography, these objective records took the form of customer sample books, trade catalogues and, more recently, 'lookbooks'. During the early days of i-D, Jones encouraged Johnston and other photographers to use only 'two frames per person', [11] not only for reasons of economy but also to encourage a sense of spontaneity. The contact sheets became works of art in their own right, with a wide range of personalities and DIY styles captured on a single grid. Jones once described them as 'sartorial police files'. [12] A series of trade cards issued by Workers For Freedom in 1985 exemplify the straight-up aesthetic, while also conjuring the stark studio backdrops of Irving Penn's portraits (75). As their name suggests, Workers For Freedom established themselves as a team operating outside the fashion mainstream – an ethos reflected in the scrawled contact details on the reverse of the cards. This rejection of mechanical typesetting was common within the world of fanzines. Barely legible handwritten titles proclaimed the avowed intention to champion bands that remained relegated to the sidelines of the mainstream music press, just as magazines such as i-D and *The Face* were providing a platform for fashion on the margins.

WORKERS FOR FREEDOM
4/4q LOWER JOHN STREET,
LONDON, WIR 3PD.
TEL: 01-734-3767
MENS AND WOMENS CLOTHING

From the very beginning, _i-D_ shared a mutual heritage with fanzines. As opposed to _The Face_'s strategy, _i-D_ was distributed through independent channels, and published with the help of Better Badges, a punk button-badge manufacturer in Portobello Road, which printed many of the key fanzines of the period. It seems natural that the graphic design sensibilities of _i-D_ should have reflected the look and feel of these renegade peer publications. The 'Fit and Form' feature juxtaposes scrawled graffiti captions with high-contrast prints and silhouettes by Katharine Hamnett, BOY and Pam Hogg (76). Jones remembers two members of his art department, Moira Bogue and Tim Hopgood, creating 'a very strong decorative identity' for _i-D_, peppering their layouts with 'fragments of handwriting using virtually any material – brush and ink, Biro, fat crayons, oil pastels, marker pens.' [13] As Bogue herself described the process, they would 'write it, swish it on the Xerox, cut it up and start again.' [14] Another common graphic device in fanzines was the use of basic typewriter text. In early issues of _i-D_, Jones used Dymo label strips and golfball typewriter heads to 'bang the text through the photographs, like a telex, to create a feeling of speed and urgency, to give an added illusion of a magazine being produced a day or two before going on sale.' [15] This technique would later be applied in the 1981 music video for Duran Duran's _Planet Earth,_ art directed by Jones's _i-D_ colleague Perry Haines, with 'ticker-tape' captions running across the screen (77).

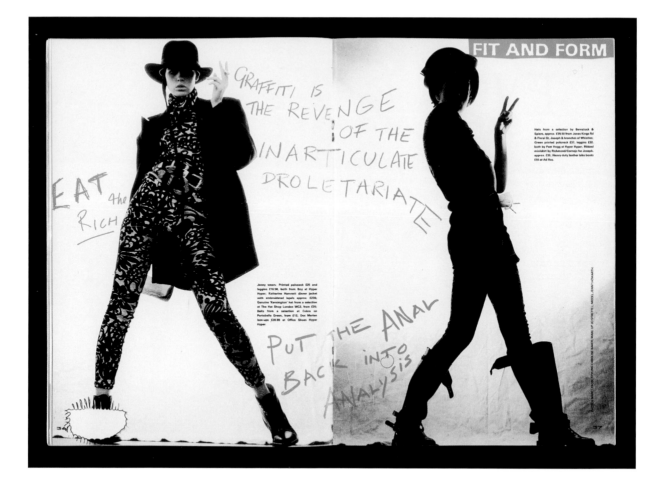

PLANET EARTH.....

UT - E

	A-001	10:02:20:24	22:54:2
⊗	E-002	13:21:14:13	13:21:1
ORT EVENT⊗	C-003		
EVENT 0002	AUX		
	BLACK		

78 ↓
*'Fourfold Summer
Survival', i-D, no.
16, May/June 1984.
Photograph by
Marc Lebon*

Jones recalls that he started using his 'cut and tear technique' at *Vogue*, where he 'had to do the fashion collections pages very fast and wanted to get a lot in – still giving the pages an impression of speed graphics.' [16] This fanzine 'cut & paste' aesthetic was given an appropriate 1980s update in an *i-D* double-page spread entitled 'Fourfold Summer Survival' (78). Here, items of clothing and style accessories from sources as diverse as Chelsea Girl, Kensington Market and Crolla are collaged together like still lifes to create bold and striking arrangements. Two years later, in an *i-D* feature entitled 'Recycled Pioneers', photographs of designs by John Galliano, Christopher Nemeth and Judy Blame were torn apart and patched together to create layered, off-centre and exaggerated forms (80). Reflecting Jones's intention to 'make design look like an accident', these images exemplify the art of the printing 'mistake'. Jones would often 'maintain trim marks, instructions, acetate overlays, tape holding down the image, in the final artwork ... asking the printer to do things they had been taught not to do.' [17] Both of these *i-D* spreads explore the concept of parallel, non-linear narratives, employing aesthetics of overlay and juxtaposition. As a comparison, the 1984 ad campaign for Joseph Tricot, art directed and photographed by Michael Roberts, featured a grid of key-lit Polaroids that resembled a cinematic storyboard sequence (80). At the other end of the spectrum, Hamza Arcan's 1987 campaign for Adel Rootstein mannequins offers similar snatched glimpses of fragmented bodies, but channelled through a rather more ruptured, dystopian narrative (81). Jones once observed that 'a magazine at its best is like a film which flows front to back and also from back to front – for the casual flipper.' [18]

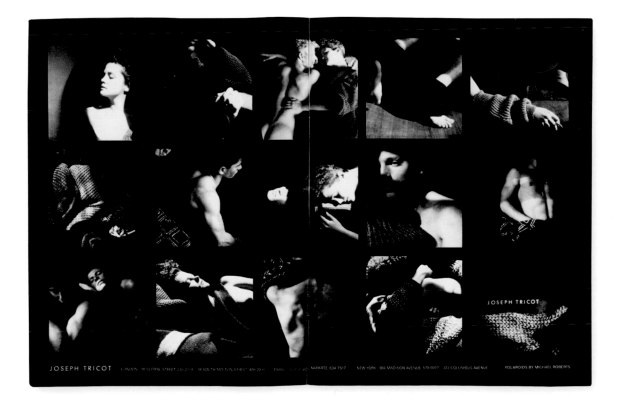

81 →
Hamza Arcan, design drawing for Adel Rootstein mannequins advertising campaign, 1987.
V&A: E.408–2012

82 →
Hyper Hyper advertisement, published in i-D, no. 20, November 1984. Art directed by Terry Jones

Jones extended his ideas to a number of contexts outside of *i-D* magazine, through his role as an image director for Fiorucci and London fashion outlet Hyper Hyper. Many of his advertising campaigns for Fiorucci and Hyper Hyper ran in *i-D* as double-page spreads or back covers (82), thus providing a prominent showcase for work that Jones described as the 'day job' while *i-D* remained the 'night job'. [19] Elio Fiorucci, who had opened his London shop in 1975 on the King's Road, wrote in 1987 about the influence that London still exerted on him: 'In the 1980s there is the same atmosphere and excitement about design as there was in the 1960s. Now when I go to London it's the same with magazines like *i-D* ... all our Italian stylists are influenced by London and our designers refer to British culture. What makes English style so special is that culture seems to occur in a bigger space in the mind ... a mixture of irony and mythology. In spite of the recession ... London is spontaneous and very much alive.' [20] These observations allude to the pluralism within style magazines such as *The Face* and *i-D*, a quality Elio Fiorucci felt personally passionate about. Writing a 1987 profile for *i-D*, Jones noted that 'Fiorucci is the whole world, the whole twentieth century in one place', further adding that for years Elio Fiorucci had 'refused to advertise, feeling at odds with the notion of promotion ... but [he] still maintains that he is selling ideas not clothes.' [21] This chimed with Jones, who had once commented that 'graphics and its solutions are influenced by the mass of ephemera in life and society.' [22] During his time as image director for Fiorucci, Jones employed photographers who were also contributors to *i-D* magazine, such as Nick Knight and Marc Lebon. Jones and Knight collaborated on a three-part series of ads for Fiorucci in 1985 that expanded upon Jones's experiments at *i-D* with coarse printing and moiré patterns. Knight's images used projected logos and negative printing colour separations, which were then transferred and manipulated on an early Scitex scanner (83).

Jones often used photocopying techniques to give photographs a harder contrast and an enlarged texture, flirting with an aesthetic that revealed a direct lineage from fanzines. The inherent qualities of layering and masking within the photocopied image were sometimes used as part of a self-reflexive strategy. In *i-D* no. 8 (the 'True Brit' issue) layers of photocopied images taken from the history of fashion were torn, peeled and enlarged to create a background texture for a contemporary street fashion photo shoot. A continuation of this appeared in the

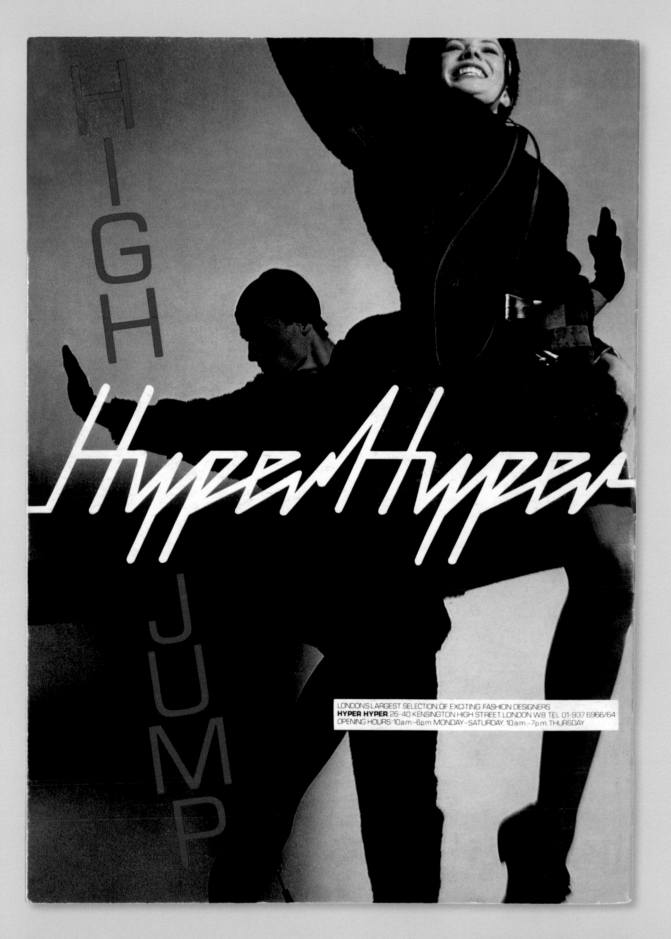

LONDON'S LARGEST SELECTION OF EXCITING FASHION DESIGNERS
HYPER HYPER 26-40 KENSINGTON HIGH STREET. LONDON W8. TEL 01-937 6966/64
OPENING HOURS: 10am-6pm MONDAY-SATURDAY. 10am-7pm. THURSDAY

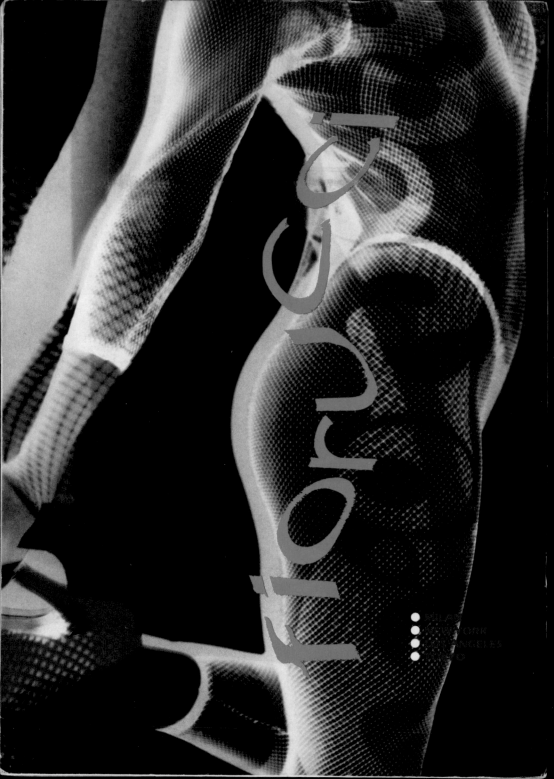

fiorucci

MILAN
NEW YORK
LOS ANGELES
TOKYO

1986 'Sicilian Freedom Fighters' feature, where Jones deemed the existing backdrop 'too clean'. Instead, a backdrop texture mash was created using enlarged photocopies of straight-up street fashion photographs taken from early issues of i-D (84).

The Face's visual identity was defined by Neville Brody, a designer brought in by Nick Logan during the early years of the magazine. Brody started his career designing record sleeves for labels such as Stiff Records and design collectives such as Rocking Russian. Brody worked at *The Face* from 1981 to 1986 and became one of the most influential graphic designers of the 1980s. In the light of Jones's self-conscious use of early i-D street fashion photographs, it is interesting to note Brody's observation that *The Face* eventually 'became witness to the death of street style … as part of the transition from low-budget culture to the multinational version

of "Youth Culture".' [23] According to Brody, *The Face* allowed photographers a free hand rather than heavily adapting their work. 'We did not want the photographs to become subservient to the identity of the magazine'. [24] He also recalls their desire to avoid the 'punk quality of photomontage'. [25] Nevertheless, the August 1984 issue shows Brody revelling in the creative potential of the aforementioned printing 'mistake'. In a feature on synthetics, Sheila Rock's photograph has been stretched and warped so that the model's Crolla shirt and spiky hair seem to reach out over the page gutter to touch the opposite side of the double spread (85). The situation at i-D seemed much more clear-cut, as Marc Lebon recalls: 'I think of myself as someone who re-presents. The clothes, models and stylists – they're the cake, the content – and the artistry of photography is only the icing, bottom of the list – Terry taught me not to be too precious.' [26]

85 →
'Synthetics',
The Face, no. 52,
August 1984. Styling
and photograph by
Sheila Rock

86 ↓
i-D, no. 21,
December 1983/
January 1984.
Backdrop by Ian
Johnstone Webb,
styling by Caroline
Baker, photograph
by Mario Testino

87 ↓
'Clash of the Tartans', _The Face_, no. 44, December 1983. Backdrop by Assorted Images, styling by Scott Crolla, photograph by Jamie Morgan

88 ↘
Malcolm Garrett (for Peter Saville Associates), record sleeve for _Dazzle Ships_ by OMD, 1983. V&A: E.2283–1990

The increasing prominence of the stylist is evident in a number of fashion features where outside collaborators were vital to the mise-en-scène. In 1984, Caroline Baker styled a Mario Testino photo shoot for _i-D_ where an abstract backdrop painted by Ian Johnstone Webb provided a suitable foil to Hilde Smith's textured, layered print patterns for Bodymap (86). The 1983 'Clash of the Tartans' feature for _The Face_ incorporated a graphically-striking background rendered in vivid colours by Assorted Images, the design group co-founded by Malcolm Garrett. This lurid re-interpretation of tartan patterns echoed Garrett's own record sleeve design work, most notably his dramatic colour-blocking for the OMD album _Dazzle Ships_, itself inspired by the dazzle camouflage developed by Vorticist painter Edward Wadsworth (87, 88).

the love-in issue

i-D

July 1985   £1.00

the indispensable document
of fashion style & ideas

KISS THIS

Street Wise And Looking Kool

89 ↙
i-D, front cover, no.
27, July 1985. Styling
by Caroline Baker,
photograph by
Robert Erdman

90 ↘
Timney Fowler
textiles, *i-D*,
no. 16, May/June
1984. Modelled by
Kate Garner, styling
by Caroline Baker,
photograph by
Cameron McVey

The Testino photo shoot and 'Tartans' feature showcase the ability of fashion stylists to produce one-off creations that exist in a single moment, specifically for the pages of a magazine. Rather like the experience of a catwalk presentation, these style spreads were bespoke commissions that relied on collaboration and operated within the constraints of the printed page to produce something that was difficult to re-create in any other context. This experiential and performative nature of style magazines was evoked by the sociologist Dick Hebdige, who observed in 1985 that *The Face* was 'not read so much as wandered through.' [27] An *i-D* feature from 1984, masterminded by Caroline Baker, typifies the spirit of the 'one-off creation'. Photographer Cameron McVey captures model Kate Garner swaddled in layered strips of Timney Fowler textiles, which have been manipulated by Baker into a bespoke body wrap (90). The article included instructional cut-and-fold diagrams for the reader. Baker was also responsible for the July 1985 *i-D* cover that featured a piece of jersey fabric, sourced from Joseph Pour La Maison, customized to work as a head wrap (89). The assemblage cleverly maintained the tradition of the famous *i-D* cover 'wink'.

The same month as their Timney Fowler collaboration, McVey and Garner appeared together in a feature for *The Face* entitled 'Style Shows a Leg', photographed by Jamie Morgan (91). McVey and Morgan were key members of the Buffalo crew, led by stylist Ray Petri, who was also responsible for this particular photo shoot. Petri cast the net far and wide for this style feature, going to Bodymap, Lillywhites and Oxfam shops to find the right look. In one photograph, Garner is pictured in a plastic bag improvising as a coat, while photographers Morgan and McVey appear themselves as models. Summing up the Buffalo philosophy, the photographs were accompanied by the following statement: 'The look is minimal, monochrome and sexy. Trash the fluorescents, flash your legs! Read these pages as IDEAS rather than designer garments.' Described as 'a gang of idealistic young hedonists' who went on to become 'international style terrorists', the Buffalo collective also included stylist Mitzi Lorenz and photographer Marc Lebon, both of whom regularly contributed to *The Face* and *i-D*. Petri, who had started at teen magazine *Honey*, recalls Buffalo 'starting as an umbrella ... collecting different people with similar ideas all in one place.' [28] Adopting the philosophy of 'non-fashion with a hard attitude', Petri's articulation of the Buffalo style relied on juxtaposition, a vital skill for any stylist. As editor Dylan Jones noted, 'no-one juxtaposed with greater aplomb than Ray ... ideas were formed on the street, not in a fashion editor's office ... the Buffalo look went beyond style into attitude.' [29] Revealing a spirit of irreverence and improvization shared with other stylists such as Baker, Petri stated: 'I don't think that fashion is that important – style is important ... you can't create a new look just by sticking someone in a new Bodymap shirt.' [30] The fashion illustrator Tony Viramontes was another member of the Buffalo circle. He collaborated with Petri on the 1985 'Body Rock' feature for *The Face*, adding playful hand-drawn flourishes to animate his own photographs with bespoke embellishments (92).

91 →
'Style Shows a Leg',
<u>The Face</u>, no. 49,
May 1984. Modelled
by Kate Garner, Jamie
Morgan and Cameron
McVey, styling by Ray
Petri, photograph by
Jamie Morgan and
Cameron McVey

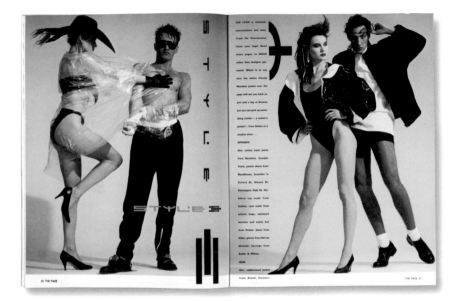

92 →
'Body Rock',
<u>The Face</u>, no. 65,
September 1985.
Styling by Ray Petri,
photograph and
illustration by Tony
Viramontes

Neville Brody's influence was most apparent through his innovations in typography. The typefaces that he introduced at *The Face* exhibited a rigid geometric quality, almost dictatorial in nature. Drawing a parallel between the social climate of the 1930s and that of the 1980s, Brody's graphic strategy highlighted what he summarized as 'the divided nation, the class division, the economic recession and a highly authoritarian government.' [31] However, the geometry also allowed for flexibility, enabling Brody to playfully subvert its assertive form. This would often result in individual letters being mutated and separated from the rest of a word. This was especially noticeable in the visual treatment of the word 'STYLE' within *The Face*'s fashion pages, where the letters 'Y' and 'E' would appear enlarged like isolated architectural fragments. It wasn't long before advertisers identified this aesthetic as a key look for the period, and began to appropriate Brody's techniques. Writing in 1987, John Hegarty, of advertising giants Bartle Bogle Hegarty, offered this rather honest assessment: 'Most of what you read in these magazines is unreadable, but the message is not what you say, but how you look. They have been revolutionary and we have been trying to adapt what they have been doing, to advertising.' [32] Indeed, two years before, BBH had made a commercial star of Buffalo crew member Nick Kamen, with the iconic 'Launderette' advertisement for Levi's 501 jeans. According to Brody, 'problems arose when advertisers started to emulate the layout of *The Face,* so at times the situation became very confusing … people were unable to separate the dynamism I was trying to achieve, and advertising's pastiche of it.' [33] Soon, this appropriation spread to the High Street. In the autumn of 1985, Harvey Nichols opened a specialist youth fashion department, Zone, in response to a rapidly expanding 'style' sector (93).

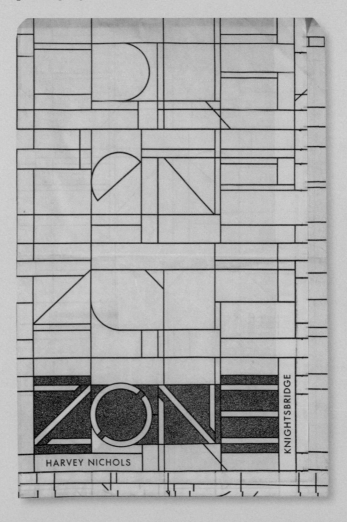

It is interesting to note that Zone's graphic identity bears striking similarities to Brody's own explorations of abstracted type and grid layouts at *The Face*. At the time, Brody described 'modern, trendy' High Street fashion shop typography as 'hollow ... it has connotations, but it isn't actually saying anything – it merely signifies'. [34] He went on, 'I wanted people to emulate the breaks with tradition that I was making ... but I didn't just want people to copy examples I'd chosen to use.'

In 1987, Brody became art director for Nick Logan's new men's title, *Arena*. Aimed at male readers who had 'grown out of *The Face*', [35] this magazine was packaged as a more commercially focused proposition. Brody established a clean look with an elegant use of white space to articulate confidence. Echoing the modernist photography of Steichen and Horst, the pages of *Arena* promoted a 'crisp attention to the detail, weave and contour of fabric', [36] resulting in monumental images that distilled clothes down to an architectural silhouette (94). It is possible that Logan's experience at *Arena* was similar to that of Terry Jones at *Vogue* during the 1970s, when the challenge lay in harnessing the photographer's creative autonomy to the demands of advertisers and designers alike. However, during a sweetly brief period in the 1980s when they remained truly independent publications, *The Face* and *i-D* existed as magazines that could offer photographers, stylists and art directors relative freedom, both in terms of subject matter and the way they represented fashion. Channelling the 'irony and mythology' of London that Elio Fiorucci loved so much, these young creatives emerged from the shadow of punk to capture the essence of club culture and street style in order to reconsider the possibilities of what a fashion magazine could be.

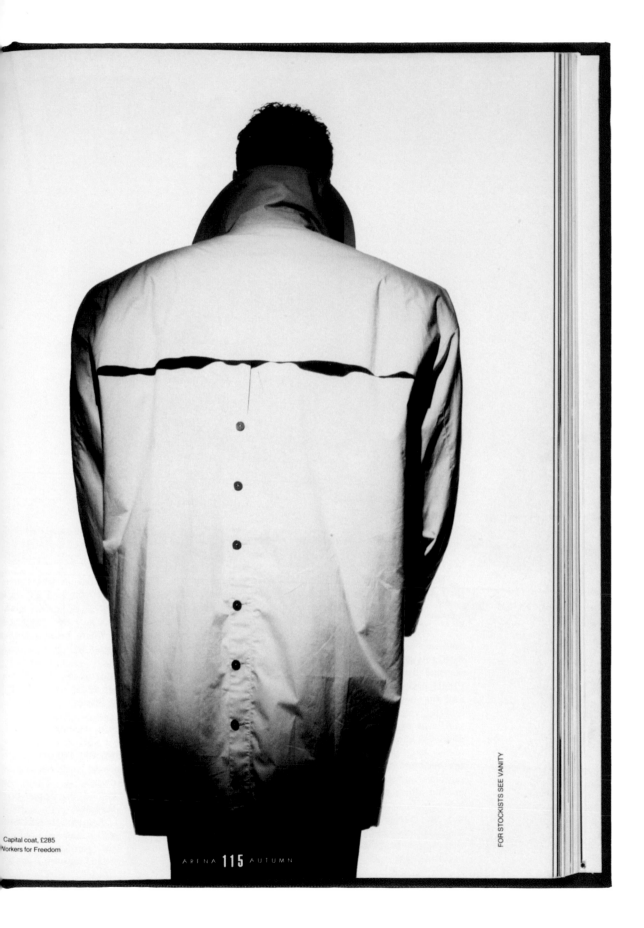

Capital coat, £285
Workers for Freedom

ARENA **115** AUTUMN

Daniel Milford-Cottam

Although first produced in London in 1921 and always a steady seller, the Filofax personal organizer established its presence on the mass market during the 1970s just in time to become an essential accessory for the 1980s high achiever. Filofax's quality leather organizers, such as the 'Winchester', were sold in distinctive boutiques such as Paul Smith's London shop, as well as department stores around the world. The Filofax became a cult object implying an extensive contact list and a demanding schedule. When paired with an expensive, status fountain pen, such as the Montblanc Meisterstück 149, and one of the early mobile phones, the 1980s professional was accessorized to suggest keen business acumen. This was important at a time when commercial success and entrepreneurialism were celebrated and esteemed.

FILOFAX

95
*Filofax 'Winchester' personal organizer
and Montblanc Meisterstück 149 pen, 1990.
V&A: T.193–1990; T.215&A–1990*

Paul Bernstock and Thelma Speirs founded Bernstock Speirs in 1982. Their designs were influenced by London's underground music and club scene, and became popular with a young clientele. Intended to be worn on a day-to-day basis, rather than saved for formal occasions, Bernstock Speirs often challenged tradition by reinterpreting classic hats in unexpected colours and/or fabrics, such as the felt pork-pie hat remade in black straw with large 'bites' taken out of it to reveal a bright orange straw lining, or deliberately crumpled trilby hats. Their 'Act Sexy' collection of Spring/Summer 1990 featured a baseball cap, its normally firm construction interpreted in soft, unstructured black cotton jersey, with a stiff, glossy peak of black and white vinyl pieced together in an undulating curve.

BERNSTOCK SPEIRS

96
Bernstock Speirs, 'Porkpie' hat and 'Act Sexy'
baseball cap, Spring/Summer 1990.
V&A: T.165–1990; T.166–1990. Given by Bernstock Speirs

PAUL SMITH

97 ↗
Paul Smith in his office, 2011. Photograph by James Mooney, courtesy of Paul Smith

SMITH

I started my business in the 1970s (I think my first collection was in 1976 or 1977) in a very humble way. Slowly, I managed to save a little money to start my own shop, which was a very, very, tiny little space about three metres square. I called it a shop but it was a windowless room.

To earn money, I worked Monday, Tuesday, Wednesday and Thursday doing freelance styling, designing fabrics, designing many things, and then on Friday and Saturday I opened my shop. After a few years I made a small collection. Actually, it was Pauline, my wife, who designed the first few collections. She's ex-Royal College of Art and trained as a fashion designer. So she was in fact my teacher. I never had any formal training.

The first collection was clothes for men: just two jackets, three shirts and a couple of sweaters.

My business has always been very gentle, growing slowly, never like a rocket, always living within my means, never borrowing large sums of money, very content with my lot. Pauline and I have been together for quite a long time. Whereas some young designers were borrowing a lot of money or getting backed by large companies, we were never like that. So the transition from the 1970s to the 1980s – we almost didn't notice it. But by that time, the difference was I didn't just have a shop in my hometown of Nottingham. I had a shop in Floral Street in Covent Garden, London, which I opened in the winter of 1979. By the time I got into the 1980s that shop had started to be a little bit settled in, a little bit well known with a certain group of people: young architects, graphic designers, musicians, quite a creative group. The shop was designed in a very minimal way – it was probably one of the first minimalist shops in all of London because it was before Issey Miyake, Yohji and Comme des Garçons came to Europe – and it attracted a lot of attention because it was in Covent Garden.

Covent Garden was EMPTY. There were no other shops at all. There were two pubs, two fruit and vegetable stalls, a ballet school, and virtually nothing else. Everything else had closed in the 1970s, when the fruit and veg market moved away. So it was this sort of little oasis in the middle of an area that had been so full of hustle bustle. I chose the location because it was the only place I could afford and also because I liked the character of Covent Garden.

I had had the opportunity to travel to Barcelona, Paris and New York, and I could draw parallels with Las Ramblas, Les Halles and SoHo, where, like all major cities, the shift goes from the centre and slowly radiates out. If you look at London today, you don't think anything of including Brick Lane, Clerkenwell and Dalston. Covent Garden was really an outback at the time but it felt good, it felt new, it felt very young. Most people thought I was mad coming here and said, 'You know, you'll never do any business' and 'It'll never happen' and 'You'll need a passport to go to Covent Garden, it's SO far out!'

The only reason the shop survived was because I still had this principle in my head of earning money by doing lots of things – my shop was an ALSO thing. I had always earned my money this way, and the shop was a piece of purity. No compromise. Unfortunately, at that time in the early 1980s, there were lots of fantastic designers in London with great ideas, very innovative, but with no business sense or backing. They relied on these quite niche collections of ideas, which often sadly weren't that well made, and so they fell by the wayside. I survived because of this dual role: earning money and having the purity of my shop.

The only way I managed to do it was to buy stock fabrics that were literally on a shelf somewhere, and they were often very, very classical fabrics. As I could only buy basic materials, I realized that in order to sell a plain white shirt, it had to have a point of view. And the point of view was a coloured button, or a coloured buttonhole or a piece of Liberty print (which I could buy from a shop, not wholesale) just under the cuff. That's really how the Paul Smith style came about. Perhaps over-described now, it is 'classic with a twist'. With Paul Smith you always get something very wearable but you also get the unexpected. This jacket I'm wearing is navy blue but has a very, very bright lining, the pockets have a very bright lining, the shirt is plain white but has snaps like a cowboy shirt.

I think one of the things I've been lucky, or just fortunate, enough to work out is the balance between selling to shops around the world, having my own shop, and my freelance work.

98 →
Paul Smith, checked wool jacket, striped cotton shirt, silk tie and corduroy trousers, Autumn/ Winter 1986. GQ, July 1986. Photograph by Denis Piel

The fabric was always from London-based stock houses. I think most of it was British-made. And it was always classical. So it would be navy-and-white striped shirting, or a white fabric, or a pale blue fabric. That was in the 1970s. With the 1980s, I started to get a little bit of a business, very tiny, so I was in a position where I could start to go to a few fabric manufacturers and ask them if maybe they would supply me. Small amounts, but still acceptable to them. A lot of it was to do with pleading and my communication skills, really!

Three things happened in the early 1980s. My first shop in 1979 was at 44 Floral Street. Then in 1982 the shop next door became available, so I managed to get that. Another thing was The Big Bang. The whole Yuppie, big-change-in-the-City, thing. A lot of the young guys with some money started buying from me. My history has been tailoring, and suits. That's my skill. Even though I now make clothes for women, it's based on a very masculine look. So I started making suits with colourful linings, or in a Prince of Wales check with a pale blue or lemon in it.

The third thing that happened was that I was approached by a Japanese man who was a scout for young European talent. He had been looking in Italy, France and Britain and he selected one designer from each country to focus on. I was the one from England. I was lucky enough to be chosen to go to Japan to meet the company and see if there was any possibility of working together. At that time a lot of young designers from around the world were being invited to go to Japan. And, in my opinion, a lot of them got it very wrong because they thought these were the heady days of Japan, there was lots of cash, and you only needed to go over once or twice. You'd send your video of your fashion show, if you had one, or you'd send some of your designs twice a year, and miraculously it would all turn into lots of cash. And some of them went up really quickly and opened three or four shops, but then also went down really quickly. Many of these young designer brands were in and out within two to four years. The difference for me was that I was actually so flattered

to be invited to this place called Japan, which seemed so far away and somewhere that I never imagined I would be able to get to, that when I was asked – even though it was by economy via Anchorage with my very, very long legs, very short seats and an 18-hour journey – I was just excited to go.

So the 1980s were very much about having a second shop in London, the Yuppie factor and more people being used to travel. Low-cost packaged tours had started to become the norm, and people felt more at ease going to other countries. Because they had been to Italy, or Spain, and had seen these perfectly nice young guys wearing these colourful things, suddenly, young men in Britain were realizing that if you wore a colourful sweater, or a colourful tie, actually it was alright!

And of course last, but not least, there was the onslaught of youth magazines, magazines that were very different from those your parents had looked at. So that was a big change as well.

I think one of the things I've been lucky, or just fortunate, enough to work out is the balance between selling to shops around the world, having my own shop, and my freelance work. Until quite recently, I've never NOT done some freelance work. So there was this stream of income: from freelance design, or fabric design, or styling. And I'd got my shop, my wholesale business. Although money was tight, I managed to keep a flow of cash coming in.

With regard to my selling in Japan, a lot of people often asked me if it was because I was British, was that the appeal? Now people ask me, is it Britishness that works for you? And the answer is I don't know. I think it was a combination of hard work, quirkiness, clothes that were wearable but had a point of view. I often describe my work as Savile Row meets Mr Bean – I never take myself too seriously. But I do understand how things are cut. I understand about proportions, make and quality, and I've always insisted on good quality. So I think it was a melange of things that helped my work in Japan, and

New combinations: the
English mix of check
stripes. *This page,* wool s
about $325; cotton dress s
$105; cotton-corduroy pa
$100; silk-brocade tie, abo
by Paul Smith. Glasses at M
Frederics Opticians, about
outfit by Azzed

Chambray with tweed. *Opp*
herringbone wool sport
$225; wool-flannel pants,
both by Calvin Klein. Cott
Calvin Klein Jeans,
Leather loafers by Char
Monsieur, about $150.
nylon socks by Interwoven
Leather belt by Polo/R
Leathergoods, about $50.
square by Gianfranco F
$16. (Hair: Thom Priano
N.Y.C. Makeup: Lind

This page, distinctive Harris tweed and an inventive young British designer team up to cut a great neotraditionalist figure. This is pattern-mixing at its best.... Three-button herringbone wool Harris-tweed sport coat, about $475; mini-checked wool vest, about $150; bold-striped cotton shirt, about $130; floral-patterned silk tie, about $50; cotton trousers, about $105: all by Paul Smith. Leather slip-ons, Aldo Brué by Nancy Knox, about $195. *Opposite* page, a modern adaptation of the Victorian salon style—a tuxedo-inspired jacket and dress shirt paired with very Holmesian checked trousers.... Short-waisted three-button wool jacket with velvet collar, about $410; silk shirt with silk appliqué front, about $260; wool trousers, about $285; leather belt, about $68: all by Workers for Freedom. Her shirt and skirt by Jasper Conran. (Hair and makeup: Susan Houser for International Artists Management, Inc., N.Y.C.)

I was probably the only one doing more classical suits, tailored but with this twist, so I think the suit was the big selling point. I still sell a very large quantity of suits today, to 76 countries. So the suit established me early on.

an ability to communicate, since most of the people I was meeting didn't speak English. Keep your sentences short, don't use any jargon, use your hands a lot! You had to find a way to make it work. When I first went to Japan in 1982, at the company I went to there was just one young man (he is still with me today) who spoke a little bit of schoolboy English. It was very much about communicating through body language, through humour, hopefully knowing your stuff, and also trying to understand things from their perspective. A lot of people are intolerant of local ways. One expression that has been helpful to me is, 'Think Global, Act Local'. I started my first shop in Japan in 1984. The interesting thing about that relationship was that I was getting a small amount of money each year from Japan as a straight fee. Then eventually it became a royalty. It was very small, but at least it was there, and it was a safety valve, a foundation for my business. I was also bringing lots of things back from Japan, which really enhanced my Covent Garden store: all the gadgets, gizmos and Boys Toys that at that time you couldn't buy in Europe, or anywhere else. Of course, I was bringing them back in suitcases, and hoping I didn't have a problem at customs, though occasionally I did! But mostly I got away with bringing back funny matt black clocks, or calculators, or cameras, or something like that, which I would then put into my shop – and that was another enhancer of Paul Smith.

Because my shop looked special, because it didn't have just clothes, and as people came to London from America or from France, that opened doors for me with Barneys and Neiman Marcus in New York, and Bon Marché in Paris. Suddenly people had found this little shop in Covent Garden, with its minimal design, concrete floors, white walls and black rails, which had all these amazing things that you couldn't find anywhere else. And, of course, I was the pioneer of the Filofax, I reintroduced boxer shorts, all in wacky colours, so I was very interesting to a lot of stores around the world. I sold to Barneys from 1979. And I still sell to Barneys. I haven't missed a season with them. Originally that was because of the Covent Garden shop, and later because I was getting an international reputation.

I think the fact that I was a young designer, who could make good tailored suits, was unique. Most of the young designers at the time, in the early 1980s, were coming

out of punk. It was more New Romantics, it was the big club scene, it was basically quite casual. So there was a lot of cotton drill, a lot of floaty fabrics, and a lot of printed cottons. I was probably the only one doing more classical suits, tailored but with this twist, so I think the suit was the big selling point. I still sell a very large quantity of suits today, to 72 countries. So the suit established me early on.

In 1978-9, British designers tended just to have little shops in the United Kingdom. In time, a lot of these designers started to come to Covent Garden. And sadly they didn't last very long, not through any fault of their own but because the landlord would only give them a three-year lease, or a five-year lease, and then the rents went higher and higher as the area became more and more popular with visitors to London. So a number of very interesting young designers came, and then went. Somehow I managed to stay. But more than that, in a very humble way, I started doing fashion shows in Paris. My first fashion show was in a friend's apartment with about 35 people in the audience, the 12 models were friends, no charge. The champagne wasn't really champagne; it was something bubbly from a supermarket. The chairs were rented. Pauline and I literally organized the whole show ourselves. The music was provided by the hi-fi system we'd brought from home, using a cassette tape that had been recorded by me using a deck and singles, so it was really hands on. And there are many cool young designers who are still very hands on. But the perception with a lot of them is that you get some money, you put on a fashion show, you get a press office and you market – and that is, of course, delightful, but my advice would be get a foundation first, and then do things gently. If you have a foundation, you can build on that.

I moved down to London in the 1970s, my wife is a Hammersmith girl born and bred, so I hope that means I'm a London designer. I have 210 staff here in London but still have almost 400 staff in Nottingham, where all the warehousing, distribution and pattern-making is done because overheads are so much higher in London. We have shops in New York, Los Angeles, Las Vegas, Paris, Milan, San Francisco and Singapore, so perhaps I'm now considered more of an international designer. But we've grown very carefully, organically and solidly. I feel privileged today to say we're very safe and sound.

Introduction

1 Kennedy Fraser, *The Fashionable Mind: Reflections on Fashion 1970–1981* (New York 1981), pp.190–1.

2 Author interview with Wendy Dagworthy, 30 November 2012.

3 Institutions from a wider hinterland, such as Birmingham College of Art and Glasgow School of Art, were also training a new generation of fashion designers, many of whom then gravitated to London to work.

4 Author email correspondence with Philip Hoare, 14 February 2012. It is worth adding his recollection of the shop interior from this same correspondence: 'It is interesting to see Modern Classics as an installation, rather than a boutique, in the manner of McLaren/Westwood's Let It Rock/ Seditionaries and stores such as Acme Attraction's Boy, and PX. The Modern Classics window displayed no clothes, just a three-dimensional curtain of tiny lead crosses suspended by nylon line. Inside, the floors were bare wood, and clothes hung as much as samples on rails as items to be bought off the peg. The idea was for customers to select a style and order clothes to be custom-made.'

5 For a detailed summary of the development of London Fashion Week, see Robert O'Byrne, *Style City: How London Became a Fashion Capital* (London 2009).

6 *Independent*, 9 March 1990.

7 *San Francisco Chronicle*, 12 March 1990.

8 Ohio's *Plain Dealer*, 23 March 1989.

9 *Sunday Oklahoma*, 22 June 1986.

10 *Dallas Morning News*, 9 April 1986.

11 Margaret Thatcher, *Margaret Thatcher: The Downing Street Years*, (London 1993). p.345.

12 *Rocky Mountain News*, 21 April 1985.

13 Author interview with Betty Jackson, 18 March 2011.

14 Ibid.

15 Author interview with Michael Costiff, 9 March 2011.

16 Author interview with Paul Smith, 12 April 2012.

17 Author interview with Stephen Jones, 17 May 2011.

18 *Harpers & Queen*, July 1983, p.87.

19 *Guardian*, 19 January 1984.

20 Rebecca Arnold, *Fashion, Desire and Anxiety* (London 2001), p.84.

21 *International Herald Tribune*, 14 March 1989.

22 *Toronto Star*, 23 March 1989.

23 British *Vogue*, May 1984, p.238.

24 The full editorial read, 'If you had a shirt with a pie-crust frill, a sprigged floral cotton skirt, a sweater tossed around the shoulders and a pair of leather loafers with gilt chain trim, then you had it all. Odd, really, that this happened at a time when British fashion was at its most individual and eccentric since the Sixties ... Sloanes are fine, particularly if they are seen and not heard. The point is not money, it is breeding and breeding alone. Breeding means inheriting the right silver, going to the right schools, using the right forks. It has very little to do with personality, individuality or talent. Elle believes that the time has come to Stamp out Sloanes' (British *Elle*, November 1985, p.14).

25 The rate of the pound to the dollar in 1985 was £0.77141; in 1988 this rate was £0.56137. Source: http://fx.sauder. ubc.ca/etc/USDpages.pdf, compiled by Professor Werner Antweiler, University of British Columbia (accessed March 2012).

New Styles New Sounds: Clubbing, Music and Fashion in 1980s London

1 Janice Miller, *Music and Fashion* (Oxford 2011), p.115.

2 Patrizia Calefato, *The Clothed Body* (Oxford 2004), pp.117, 121.

3 Sarah Thornton, *Club Cultures: Music, Media and Subcultural Capital* (Cambridge 1995), p.3.

4 See Ted Polhemus, *Streetstyle* (London 1994); Amy de la Haye and Cathie Dingwall, *Surfers Soulies Skinheads & Skaters: Subcultural Style from the Forties to the Nineties* (London 1996); and Ken Gelder (ed.), *The Subcultures Reader* (London 1995).

5 Cited in Graham Smith and Chris Sullivan, *We Can Be Heroes: London Clubland 1976–1984* (London 2011), p.46.

6 David Johnson, '69 Dean Street', *The Face*, no. 34, February 1983, p.27.

7 Cited in *The Face*, no. 46, February 1984.

8 Martin Stokes (ed.), *Ethnicity, Identity and Music: The Musical Construction of Place* (Oxford 1994), p.5.

9 Stevie Stewart, interview with author, 17 April 2012.

10 Dean Ricketts, interview with author, 22 March 2012.

11 Robert Elms, 'Nightclubbing', *The Face*, no. 100, September 1988, p.37.

12 See Dick Hebdige, *Subculture: The Meaning of Style* (London 1979) and Polhemus, *Streetstyle*.

13 Cited in David Johnson, 'Posing at the picture palace', *Evening Standard*, May 1983; http:// shapersofthe80s.com/clubbing/1983-posing-with-a-purpose-at-the-camden-palace (accessed 21 April 2012).

14 Jeffrey Hinton, interview with author, 17 April 2012.

15 Thornton, *Club Cultures*.

16 Daniel Hadley, quoted in Thornton, *Club Cultures*, p.60.

17 Le Palace was described by Roland Barthes in *Vogue Hommes* in 1978 as 'not a simple enterprise but a work' with 'a whole apparatus of sensations destined to make people happy, for the interval of a night' (Roland Barthes, *Incidents* [Berkeley, Calif. 1992], p.48).

18 Robert Elms, 'Hard Times', *The Face*, no. 29, September 1982, p.15.

19 Johnsons, owned by established outfitter and former ace mod Lloyd Johnson, had 'three quiffed mannequins in the window, one blond and the other two black-haired that I had bought in France [and] looked exactly like the three members of the American Rockabilly group The Stray Cats' (Lloyd Johnson, interview with author, 16 March 2012).

20 Anon, 'NightClubbingNightClubbingNightClubbing', *New Sounds New Styles*, July 1981, p.26.

21 Anon, 'i-D Talks to Kate, Paul and Jeremiah (Haysi Fantayzee)', *i-D*, no. 10, 1980, p.30.

22 Cited in Helen Roberts, 'The Individual Clowes Show', *The Face*, no. 29, September 1982, p.40.

23 Kasia Maciejowska, *The House of Beauty and Culture: A Provisional Investigation* (RCA/V&A MA History of Design, 2011), unpublished thesis, p.177.

24 Alex Sharkey, 'Black Market', *i-D*, no. 48, June 1987, p.96.

25 Anon, 'The Appropriators', *i-D*, no. 48, June 1987, p.53.

26 The Fridge was owned by Andrew Czezowski, who had formerly run punk club The Roxy, which in 1978 became Billy's, the club where Egan and Strange held their first Bowie night.

27 Sue Tilley, *Leigh Bowery: The Life and Times of an Icon* (London 1997), pp.52–3.

28 Jeffrey Hinton, interview with author, 17 April 2012.

29 David Holah, interview with author, 17 April 2012.

30 Stevie Stewart, interview with author, 17 April 2012.

31 Cited in Tilley, *Leigh Bowery*, p.65.

32 Matthew Collin, *Altered State: The Story of Ecstasy Culture and Acid House* (London 1998).

33 Sonia Frezza, 'Back to Reality: The Soul II Soul Phenomenon', *i-D*, no. 76, December 1989, p.67.

34 Ibid.

35 Cited in Carol Tulloch, 'Rebel Without a Pause', *Chic Thrills: A Fashion Reader*, edited by Juliet Ash and Elizabeth Wilson (Berkeley, Calif. 1992), p.93.

36 London's first hip hop club, the Language Lab, was held at Gossips at 69 Dean Street. The importance of basement club Gossips, and the Gargoyle on the top floor of the same building, was charted by David Johnson in '69 Dean Street', pp.26–31.

37 Cited in Smith and Sullivan, *We Can Be Heroes*, p.198.

38 Collin, *Altered State*, p.57.

39 Ibid, p.62.

40 John Godfrey, 'The Amnesiacs', *i-D*, no. 52, June 1988, pp.66, 70.

41 Sheryl Garrett, 'Happy Happy', *The Face*, no. 98, June 1988, p.22.

42 Cited in Paul Gorman, *The Look* (London 2006), p.197.

London Calling:
Designer Fashion in 1980s London

1 *Le Soir*, 17 March 1988.

2 The event honoured the designers' donations of this material to the Museum's permanent collections.

3 Michael Costiff, interview with author, February 2011.

4 *Harpers & Queen*, December 1984, p.281.

5 British *Vogue*, July 1987, p.138.

6 Ibid.

7 *The Face*, May 1983, p.30.

8 'London Goes Wild: dazzling printmakers steal the show', *Newsweek*, 1 April 1985.

9 'English with an Eastern Accent', *Dallas Times Herald*, 19 October 1988.

10 'London Goes Wild', *Newsweek*, April 1985.

11 Wendy Dagworthy, interview with author, 30 November 2012.

12 *The Observer on Sunday*, 17 October 1982.

13 Paul Smith, interview with author, April 2012.

14 See Sandy Black's *Knitting: Fashion, Industry and Craft* (London 2012).

15 *Harpers & Queen*, September 1984, p.199.

16 Author's email correspondence with Philip Hoare, 14 February 2012.

17 'British Designers Go Indian For Summer', *Carib Daily News*, week ending 6 December 1988.

18 *San Francisco Chronicle*, 18 November 1985.

19 Wendy Dagworthy, interview with author, 30 November 2012.

20 In a 1996 interview, Howell stated that her early designs used almost all British fabrics. See Amy de la Haye, *The Cutting Edge: 50 Years of British Fashion* (London 1996), p.194.

21 Kennedy Fraser, *The Fashionable Mind* (New York 1981), p.190.

22 'London Designers Play It Safe', *Women's Wear Daily*, 15 October 1990.

23 'Vivienne Westwood: Punks, Pirates and the Queen', *Sportswear International*, March 1989, p.57.

24 *Tobé Associates Report*, Tobé Associates, New York, 21 October 1989.

NOTES

Irony and Mythology:
The Fashion Magazine Reconsidered

1 Nick Logan, quoted in Mitzi Lorenz (ed.), *Ray Petri: Buffalo* (New York 2000), p.147.

2 Interview with Nick Logan, published on music blog *Test Pressing*, 16 April 2012.

3 Lorenz, *Ray Petri*, p.147.

4 Ibid.

5 Logan, *Test Pressing*.

6 Dylan Jones, quoted in Terry Jones (ed.), *Smile i-D: Fashion and Style – The Best from 20 Years of i-D* (London 2001), p.9.

7 Terry Jones, quoted in T. Jones, *Catching the Moment* (London 1997), p.40.

8 Ibid.

9 Isabelle Anscombe, *Not Another Punk Book!* (London 1978), p.71.

10 Jones, *Catching the Moment*, p.168.

11 Jones, *Smile i-D*, p.23.

12 Ibid.

13 Terry Jones, *Instant Design: A Manual of Graphic Techniques* (London 1990).

14 Ibid.

15 Ibid.

16 Jones, *Instant Design*, p.15.

17 Ibid.

18 Ibid.

19 Interview with Terry Jones, published in online fashion magazine *Hint*, December 2005.

20 Catherine McDermott, *Street Style: British Design in the 80s* (London 1987).

21 Terry Jones profile on Elio Fiorucci, *i-D* magazine, September 1987, pp.74–7.

22 Jones, *Instant Design*, p.10.

23 Jon Wozencroft, *The Graphic Language of Neville Brody* (London 1988), p.99.

24 Wozencroft, *Graphic Language*, p.96.

25 Ibid.

26 Jones, *Catching the Moment*, p.55.

27 Dick Hebdige, 'The Bottom Line on Planet One: Squaring Up to The Face', *Ten.8* photo journal, vol. 19, 1985, p.43; cited in Paul Jobling, *Fashion Spreads: Word and Image in Fashion Photography since 1980* (Oxford 1999), p.41.

28 Lorenz, *Ray Petri*, p.157.

29 Ibid.

30 Lorenz, *Ray Petri*, p.158.

31 Wozencroft, *Graphic Language*, p.18.

32 McDermott, *Street Style*, p.83.

33 Wozencroft, *Graphic Language*, p.102.

34 Wozencroft, *Graphic Language*, p.18.

35 Ibid.

36 Ibid.

Further Reading

Hilton Als, *Leigh Bowery* (London 1998)

François Boucher, *A History of Costume in the West* (London 1996)

Christopher Breward, E. Ehrman and C. Evans (eds), *The London Look* (London 2002)

Christopher Breward and David Gilbert (eds), *Fashion's World Cities* (Oxford 2006)

Jessica Cargill Thompson and Jonathan Derbyshire (eds), *London Calling: High Art and Low Life in the Capital since 1968* (London 2008)

Stephen Colegrave and Chris Sullivan (eds), *Punk: A Life Apart* (London 2001)

Stephanie Curtis Davies, *Costume Language: A Dictionary of Dress Terms* (Malvern 1995)

Amy de la Haye, *The Cutting Edge: 50 Years of British Fashion 1947–1997* (London 1996)

Amy de la Haye and Cathie Dingwall (eds), *Surfers Soulies Skinheads and Skaters: Subcultural Style from the Forties to the Nineties* (London 1996)

Caroline Evans and Minna Thornton (eds), *Women and Fashion: A New Look* (London 1989)

Elizabeth Ewing, *History of Twentieth Century Fashion* (London 1974)

Maria Luisa Frisa, *Excess: Fashion and the Underground in the 1980s* (Milan 2004)

Paul Gorman, *The Look: Adventures in Pop and Rock Fashion* (London 2001, rev. edn 2006)

Georgina Howell, *Sultans of Style: Thirty Years of Fashion and Passion 1960–1990* (London 1990)

Paul Jobling, *Fashion Spreads, Word and Image in Fashion Photography since 1980* (Oxford 1999)

Kurt Salmon Associates, *Survey of the UK Fashion Designer Scene* (prepared for the British Fashion Council, January 1991)

Catherine McDermott, *Made in Britain: Tradition and Style in Contemporary British Fashion* (London 2002)

Catherine McDermott, *Street Style: British Design in the 80s* (London 1987)

Valerie Mendes and Amy de la Haye, *20th Century Fashion* (London 1999)

Jane Mulvagh, *Vogue History of 20th Century Fashion* (London 1988)

Robert O'Byrne, *Style City. How London Became a Fashion Capital* (London 2009)

Alistair O'Neill, *London: After a Fashion* (London 2007)

Ted Polhemus, *Streetstyle: From Sidewalk to Catwalk* (London 1994)

Gerry Saunders, *The UK Fashion Industry* (Emap Fashion, London, November 1998)

Jon Savage, *England's Dreaming: Sex Pistols and Punk Rock* (London 1991)

Graham Smith and Chris Sullivan, *We Can Be Heroes: London Clubland 1976–1984* (London 2011)

Neil Spencer, 'Menswear in the 1980s: Revolt into Conformity', in *Chic Thrills: A Fashion Reader*, ed. Juliet Ash and Elizabeth Wilson (London 1992; Berkeley, CA., 1996)

Valerie Steele, *Women of Fashion: Twentieth Century Designers* (New York 1994)

Andrew Tucker, *The London Fashion Book* (London 1998)

Linda Watson, *Vogue: Twentieth-Century Fashion* (London 2000)

Claire Wilcox (ed.), *Radical Fashion* (London 2001)

Claire Wilcox, *Vivienne Westwood* (London 2004)

Acknowledgements

This book's many contributors and participants deserve lavish praise. Foremost, I would like to thank the book's talented authors: Shaun Cole, Abraham Thomas, Daniel Milford-Cottam, and Paul Smith. I extend particular gratitude to Wendy Dagworthy, who infused the project with knowledge and passion. In spite of the more than usual challenges of getting a book to print, this group remained loyal and cheerful participants. I am also grateful to Annette Worsley-Taylor for planting the initial seed for this book, to the Royal College of Art for their support of Wendy's research efforts and to Hilary Laurence, the RCA's able administrator, for her continuing good humour. I would also like to thank all the designers, donors and lenders of garments and images featured in this publication.

Within V&A Publishing, Frances Ambler warrants heartfelt praise for staying the course and remaining a positive force to ensure the book's completion. I would also like thank Mark Eastment, Head of Publishing, as well as Lee Davies, Davina Cheung, Liz Edmunds, Vicky Haverson and the eagle eye and sound advice of copy-editor Denny Hemming. Many designers supported this project, in particular Fraser Taylor, Stevie Stewart, Margaret Howell and Michiko Koshino. Michael Costiff was an enthusiastic source of material and information as was Philip Hoare. Stephen Jones and Betty Jackson were both wonderful advice-givers and storytellers.

I am grateful to Furniture, Textiles and Fashion Department colleagues Christopher Wilk, Claire Wilcox and Oriole Cullen for their unwavering support and advice and to Stephanie Wood for making all requests seem reasonable. Gratitude is also extended to colleagues in the Photography Studio, including Richard Davies, Peter Kelleher and especially Jaron James for taking so many requests in his stride. To Kate Bethune, thank you for ensuring that the photography went smoothly. I also wish to recognize the contributions of Paul Gorman and Louise Rytter.

Contributor Biographies

Sonnet Stanfill is Curator of Twentieth-century and Contemporary Fashion at the V&A. She curated the displays *Ossie Clark* (2003) and *New York Fashion Now* (2007) and co-curated the exhibition *Ballgowns: British Glamour Since 1950* as well as writing the accompanying book (V&A 2012).

Shaun Cole is a writer, lecturer and curator and currently Course Director for Masters degrees in History and Culture of Fashion and Fashion Curation at London College of Fashion. He has written and lectured on the subject of menswear and gay fashion and his publications include *'Don We Now Our Gay Apparel': Gay Men's Dress in the Twentieth Century* (2000), *Dialogue: Relationships in Graphic Design* (V&A 2005) and *The Story of Men's Underwear* (2010).

Professor Wendy Dagworthy OBE formed her own company in 1972 and two years later joined the prestigious London Designer Collections, where she subsequently became Director from 1982 to 1990. After her success during the 1970s and 80s selling her collections to an international market, from 1989 she ran BA (Hons) Fashion at Central Saint Martins. She became Head of the School of Fashion & Textiles in 2000 and is now Dean of the new School of Material. A member of the British Fashion Council's Advisory Board since 1996, she was awarded an OBE in 2011 for services to the fashion industry.

Daniel Milford-Cottam is a former assistant curator in Furniture, Textiles and Fashion at the V&A. He has contributed to *The Wedding Dress: 300 Years of Bridal Fashions* (V&A 2011) and *Hats: An Anthology* (V&A 2009). He is currently a cataloguer for the Paintings, Drawings and Prints department at the V&A.

Paul Smith opened his first shop in Nottingham in 1970. He took evening classes in tailoring and developed his look with the help of his girlfriend (now wife) Pauline, an RCA graduate. In 1976 he showed his first menswear collection in Paris. Since then he has established himself as a pre-eminent British designer combining a sense of humour and mischief with a love of tradition. The unique Paul Smith shops throughout Europe, America and Asia reflect the character of Paul and his designs. Paul Smith continues to be involved with every aspect of the company both as designer and chairman.

Abraham Thomas is Curator of Designs at the V&A. He was the curator of the exhibitions *Heatherwick Studio: Designing the Extraordinary* (2012) and *1:1 – Architects Build Small Spaces* (2010). He is currently writing a book on the V&A's collection of fashion drawings and photography (forthcoming, 2014).

Image Credits

Front cover
Albert Watson / *Vogue* © The Condé Nast Publications Ltd.

Back cover
Design by Helen David for English Eccentrics

Section openers

New Styles New Sounds, pp.32–3
Left: Philip Sallon at The Mud Club, London, 1986. Photograph by David Swindells – PYMCA.com

Centre and right: Axiom fashion show at Club for Heroes, London,1981. Photograph by David Johnson/ ShapersOfThe80s

London Calling, pp.52–3
Left: Leigh Bowery ensembles in *London Goes To Tokyo* catalogue, 1984. Collection of Michael Costiff.

Centre top: Michiko Koshino ensemble, Autumn/Winter 1979. V&A: T.265-270&A-1980.

Centre bottom: The Cloth (for Betty Jackson), advertisement for Saks Fifth Avenue c.1984. Courtesy of Betty Jackson.

Right: Murray Arbeid ensemble, *Harpers & Queen*, October 1985. Photograph by Fabrizio Ferri. Courtesy of *Harper's Bazaar* (UK).

Irony and Mythology, pp.78–9
Left: *The Face*, no.65, September 1985. Styling by Ray Petri, photograph and illustration by Tony Viramontes. *The Face* Magazine / Bauer Magazine.

Centre top: 'Bottomless Wonder', *The Face*, no.60, April 1985. Styling by Caroline Baker, photograph by Andrew Macpherson. *The Face* Magazine / Bauer Magazine.

Centre bottom: 'Synthetics', *The Face*, no.52, August 1984. Styling and photograph by Sheila Rock. *The Face* Magazine / Bauer Magazine.

Right: 'Rifat Ozbek', The Face, no.74, June 1986. Styling by Sarajane Hoare, photograph and illustration by Tony Viramontes. *The Face* Magazine / Bauer Magazine.

Copyright
Designed and illustrated by Hamza Arcan 81

© Robyn Beeche 40

Courtesy of The Cloth (David Band, Brian Bolger, Helen Manning and Fraser Taylor) 52

Design by Helen David for English Eccentrics 53

CLIVE DIXON/Rex Features 27

Courtesy of EMI Records 77, 87–8

Tim Graham/Getty Images 5

Courtesy of *Harper's Bazaar* (UK) 45–6, 51, 54, 60, 64, 69, p.53

© Mr Hartnett – PYMCA.com Frontispiece, 33, 37

Courtesy of *i-D* Magazine 20, 49, 74, 76, 78–9, 82–4, 86, 89, 90

Courtesy of Betty Jackson 4, 63

David Johnson/Shapersofthe80s 22, 24, pp.32–3

Kawa/*GQ*; © Condé Nast 99

Neil Kirk/*Vogue* © The Condé Nast Publications Ltd 50

Piel/*GQ*; © Condé Nast 98

© Ted Polhemus – PYMCA.com 26

Redferns 23

© Derek Ridgers 31

Graham Smith, *We Can Be Heroes, (Punks, Poseurs, Peacocks and People of a Particular Persuasion – London Clubland 1976–83)* 19, 34

© David Swindells – PYMCA.com 29, 30, 36, 38, p.32

The Face Magazine / Bauer Media 21, 25, 80, 85, 87, 91–2, pp.78–9

Jim Varriale/*Vogue* © The Condé Nast Publications Ltd 48

Courtesy of Violette Editions 9

Index

Index